Walking With Elemental Spirits:
How to Work with Elemental Spirits and Get Consistent Results

Walking with Elemental Spirits:
How to Work with Elemental Spirits and Get Consistent Results

Taylor Ellwood

Eugene, Oregon

Walking with Elemental Spirits: How to Work with Elemental Spirits and Get Consistent Results
by Taylor Ellwood
© 2022 first edition

Cover Art: Mark Reid
Editor: Taylor Ellwood
Set in Consolas and Book Antiqua
ME0024
ISBN 9798419455528
Magical Experiments Publication
http://www.magicalexperiments.com

Other Non-Fiction Books by Taylor Ellwood

The Process of Magic
Manifesting Wealth
The Magic of Art
How to Troubleshoot your Magic
Magic by Design
The Magic of Writing
Pop Culture Magick
Pop Culture Magic 2.0
Pop Culture Magic Systems
Space/Time Magic Foundations
Space/Time Magic
Magical Identity
Inner Alchemy
Inner Alchemy of Life
Inner Alchemy of Internal Work
Inner Alchemy of Wintering
A Magical Life
Mystical Journeys
Magical Movements
A Magical Stillness
A Magical Creativity
Walking with Magical Entities
Walking with Spirits
Occult Poetics

Dedication

To the elemental spirits who have guided me and walked with me for so much of my life.

And to Jennifer Gerrity, who has shared her path with me and in the process taught me even more about how to walk with spirits.

Acknowledgements

Special thanks goes out to Kara Smith, Denny Asiedu, Bo Jacisin, Gayle Wyant, Feda Slaki, Gemma Young, and Nate Stein for submitting questions to the Q and A chapter for this book. I hope I answered your questions! I also want to thank Mark Reid for the excellent cover he's put together. Finally I want to thank all the people who've taken the time express appreciation for my work. I'm so deeply pleased that my work has helped you in your own spiritual path.

Table of Contents

Introduction

I started practicing magic when I was 16, which at the time of this writing was nearly 30 years ago. The magic I first learned was a combination of neo-shamanic techniques and elemental hermeticism that I learned about from reading Ted Andrews' books on the topics. I religiously read those books and practiced all the exercises. I wanted to practice the magic after all, because I had learned it was real.

I had wanted magic to be real for a long time. As a kid, I grew up reading the *Greek Myths 1 and 2*, as well as *The Aeneid* and *Watership Down*. For a young, impressionable mind, the stories were so rich with possibilities, and I felt a deep dissatisfaction that the world I lived in didn't seem to have magic. It should be no surprise that I plunged into reading fantasy books, as a preteen and teenager, because those books took me to worlds where magic was real, and where the mysteries of the universe were waiting to be explored. I particularly enjoyed both the Elric saga by Michael Moorcock (which in retrospect I realized played a huge role in my approach to elemental magic) and the Dragonlance saga, which featured one of my favorite fantasy magicians to this day, Raistlin Majere. I identified strongly with him, because like him, I knew what it was like to be the outsider of any group I was in. Even to this day, I still identify with him and it's fair to say that he plays a dynamic role in how I think about and practice magic.

One of the most pivotal days of my life, to this very day, happened in Mid-April of 1993. I don't remember the exact date, but I can set the rest of the scene. I was a geeky tenth grader who had no friends. I was sitting in the library reading *The Crystal Shard* by Richard Salvatore and hoping I wouldn't get picked on by the high school jocks and prep kids who always seemed on the lookout, ready to pick on the weird kid who didn't fit in and belong. Then he came into the library.

Andy Burkins. I'll never forget that name, or the person. He was taller than me, and he didn't exactly fit in either, but he was definitely higher up in the high school pecking order. He walked into the library, spotted me, and changed directions to come sit at the table I was at. I braced myself, ready to be picked on, but all he did was sit down at the table.

"I've got a story to tell you," Andy said.

"Ok," I cautiously replied, not sure what else to say and just hoping I could get back to my book of sword and sorcery.

Andy proceeded to tell me what he thought was a wild story about astral projection and encountering a demon that he fought, while he was astral projecting. A couple years later he would confess to me that he told me the story because he saw how much I enjoyed reading fantasy books and he wanted to freak me out by showing me that magic was real. Ironically, the reaction he got was the exact opposite of what he expected and hoped for.

Once he finished telling his tale, which I listened to in rapt silence, he looked over at me, with a curious expression on his face. I quietly regarded him and then I asked him one of the most important questions I've ever asked anyone.

"Where can I learn more?"

Andy gave me a startled look. It was the last thing he expected to hear.

"I can bring you some books tomorrow," he said.

"Bring them. I want to learn more about this and find out if magic is real."

Andy got up and left, but I didn't resume reading *The Crystal Shard*. Instead, I sat in the library, my mind racing with the thought, *Magic is REAL!!* I followed up that thought with, *I want to learn everything I can about magic.*

Thus I started walking the spiritual path that to this day I continue walking. The next day, Andy did bring in a couple pamphlets as well as a copy of Ted Andrew's book *How to Meet and Work with Spirit Guides*. I don't have the pamphlets any more, but I never did return *How to*

Meet and Work with Spirit Guides. It still has an honored place on my bookshelf and it has been read a few times over, the cover and pages worn by eager loving hands that wanted to plumb the depths of that book and discover the secrets of magic.

What I discovered in that book as well as the first book I actually bought, *Enchantments of the Faerie Realm*, is what I consider to be the foundational keystone of my magical practice, on which everything else has been built. I learned about the elemental spirits of the classic five Western elements, as well as the archangels. I learned about Quabalah and how to go into altered states of mind. All in all, not a bad foundation to start out with.

In the almost thirty years since I first started practicing magic, I have expanded beyond where I started, exploring the various systems of Western esotericism, ranging from ceremonial and ritual magic to chaos magic, and I have also explored Taoist and Dzogchen practices. Beyond even all of that I have integrated non-occult disciplines into my magical work, and created unique systems of magic that I have written about and will to continue write about.

But it all started with elemental magic. Even my drive to experiment with magic started with elemental magic, because within a year of reading Ted Andrews books, I began to experiment with and improve on the practices and processes that he shared, eager to test my limits and discover what I could really do with the magic.

To this day I practice elemental magic and it continues to play a significant role in my magical path and development. This book, which you hold in your hands, is the current culmination of the last 29 years of my spiritual practice with elemental magic. It is an offering of gratitude to the elemental spirits, as well as an exploration of what elemental magic and the work with the elemental spirits can become. This book is special to me, because it is the distillation of so many experiments and work that I've done with elemental magic. It is also, in the vein of all my books, an attempt to evolve the current discipline of magic, to challenge the sacred cows that are held dear, and to show you the possibilities that are waiting to be explored.

I don't presume to have all the answers. I'm not the end all, be all authority of elemental magic (or any other magic). All I offer is my voice, my perspectives and my experiences in the hope that they might inspire you just as Ted Andrews inspired me with his writing. Nonetheless, I also hope that like my younger self (and even to do this day my current self) you will also not just read this book and practice the exercises in it, but also seek to challenge my perspectives with your own work and experiences, and evolve your spiritual practice with the elements, beyond what I share in these pages. The mark of a true magician, after all, is discovered when you make what you learn your own and discover what you can do with it, beyond the wildest expectations and hopes of the author who wrote the book you are reading. The true evolution of magic, of any type, can only happen if you are willing to do the work and discover the answers to the questions that will naturally arise as you read this book and all the others you read. I urge you not to limit your answers to those questions to what is in this book, or any other occult book. Instead use this book to expand your horizons and then proceed beyond to continue your journey. If you can do that, you will not only learn what magic can truly do, but discover what you can truly become.

And now...

Let us start walking with elemental spirits.

Taylor Ellwood

Eugene, OR

May 2022

Chapter 1: What are Elemental Spirits?

As I shared in my introduction, I first started practicing elemental magic. It made a certain sense to me and it is embedded deeply in how I practice magic to this day. Yet, my practice of elemental magic has changed over the years. I initially started out practicing using the classical Western 5 elemental model of Earth, Air, Fire, Water, and Spirit (Quintessence). I eventually explored the Eastern models, which also have 5 elements, though with distinct differences. Still, I felt that there was something missing. What has always bothered me about how elemental magic is portrayed is something that bothers me about occult disciplines in general: There is a tendency to never question or explore how the occult discipline could evolve past the traditional explanations and knowledge that have been passed down from days of yore. Elemental magic is a good example of this, because elemental magic as most people know it is still based on traditional and classical notions of what the elements are.

Of course, I imagine my critics saying, if it ain't broke Taylor, why fix it? And it is true that the classic model of elemental magic is a very functional model. It works exceedingly well, so why make any changes to it, especially if there's no need for it, no glaring error, at least on the surface that calls for such a change? The problem with that perspective is that it is a complacent one, which leads to the stagnation of the occult disciplines. If we never question or examine or experiment with a given occult discipline, we ultimately settle for less because we are choosing to stop ourselves at a place that is defined by someone else (in this case long dead), instead of exploring what the work could be. Now that is a presumptuous statement of me to make, because a person's spiritual path is ultimately their own and how someone works with the elements or any other aspect of magic is going to differ to some degree on the basis of the work they are engaged in. Nonetheless I make that statement because there are occult disciplines where there is very little public progress in changing that occult discipline and a lot of resistance to such changes, because of how those changes are perceived. I see this in the glut of books that are currently available on working with elemental spirits. There is a lot of material that essentially rehashes standard elemental magic theory and practice. In fairness, some of that material does offer some new perspectives and takes on the existing theory of elemental magic, but nonetheless if I have one criticism of all those books and indeed elemental magic and spirit work in general it is that magicians have failed to step out of the shadow of the past and discover what else elemental magic could be. This book is an attempt at stepping past the conventional theory and practice of working with elemental spirits and magic. In order to do that though, we must first look at the actual foundation of elemental magic as well as what we traditionally consider to be elemental spirits.

What are Elemental Spirits?

The core of Western elemental magic is focused on working with elemental spirits. As I mentioned above there are 5 elements: Earth, Air, Fire, Water, and Spirit (Quintessence). These five elements exist in all things, including ourselves, to some degree or another. They are essential to life, because of what they represent:

> Elementals are building blocks of nature. They are close to being true energy and consciousness, and they have not developed enough to truly take on personality. When we are in contact with them, they stimulate strong, definable responses in us. These responses are characterized by labeled with an elemental designation - earth, water, air, and fire. Each kind of elemental reflects a basic energy pattern of the faerie realm as it builds and manifests in nature. They interweave to create and sustain all matter on Earth. All four kinds of elementals exist in every aspect of nature and in every person (Andrews 1993b, P. 33).

Andrews leaves out Spirit, but it applies to that element as much as to the others, with the understanding that Spirit, as an element, is the glue that binds the others together. Susan Raven provides further insight to what elementals are by noting the following:

> An elemental is a nexus of subtly primed consciousness and vitality working at the junction between spirit and matter. It is a constituent part of an ever-evolving, life-giving expression of divine creation, working on the front line of physical formation. Each elemental is charged with a specific mission regarding the assemblage, cohesion, and animation of physical matter on Earth, ranging from the density of mountain rock to the rarified heat of a candle flame. They are created and programmed by a sublime hierarchy of advanced consciousness, who over aeons of time developed their Life Spirit to a point where they can create life itself – and give it away! (2012, P. 46).

What we can take away from this refined definition is that elementals have very specific functions that they perform. In this, they are similar to angels and are typically thought to be in the same hierarchy (such as that is) as the angels. They perform a different function than the angels, because they are oriented toward working on the physical level of existence, helping to create and stabilize life as we know it. From a spiritual perspective, it can be claimed that the reason we have life on Earth is because of the elementals. They create the conditions that makes existence on this planet viable, because of how they balance each other and work together to build the conditions for life to flourish (Pogacnik 2009, Raven 2012). Swain notes the following about elementals: "They are very function based in terms of ordering and carrying out the functions of their elemental realms...Being elemental they are very physically concerned and are very much about clear real world manifestations" (2018 P. 79). The functional focus of the elemental spirits is to manifest the particular elemental energy they mediate and use it to bring balance to the world, but of course there is much to the elemental spirits than just this primary focus of their essence and being.

While elementals are essential to the building blocks of life, and as a consequence to our own existence, we should rightfully ask what is the benefit they derive from being in touch with us. One of the claims that I see various authors make is that the elementals evolve as a result of being in contact with humanity (Andrews 1993b, Pogacnik 2007, Pogacik 2009, Pogacnik 2016, Swain 2018, Dominguez 2021). This is a fascinating claim to make, and there may be some truth to it. Certainly, if we examine why spirits in general seem to want to connect with people, it is because we can do something for them, or provide them something that they otherwise cannot have. In turn they provide us something that we don't have access to otherwise, or at the least would be much harder to get access to. It is always useful to remember this about any given spirit. The advantage elementals have over other spirits is that they are closer to the manifest plane and have more of a direct effect on it than other types of spirits do. This is good to remember when you work with elementals, especially in terms of recognizing how they can move you, but also in terms of recognizing what you can provide to them:

> There is a strong drive toward spiritual evolution in all beings. When beings observe each other or interact with each other, both are hanged. When elementals engage with beings such as humans, that have a fourfold nature, the part of them that is the seed pattern of the other Elements is enlivened. For example, given enough time and exposure to human energy, an elemental of Water may better grasp Fire, Air, and Earth. Ritual work and magick involving the elemental spirits create opportunities for communication

and energetic exchange. The process of communication between humans and elementals is mediated through the spiritual, divine spark within in each type of being. By connecting, directly or through resonance, through the functional equivalents of each other's higher selves, each party is given exposure to the other vision of wholeness and utility (Dominguez Jr 2021 P. 42)

We mutually benefit from working with each other. The elementals gain experiences as a result of working with us that tap them into the essence of the other elements and allow them to grow beyond the initial functioning that they otherwise focus on. We, in turn, get access to the elemental energies, and come to a greater awareness of how we can achieve balance with that elemental energy (I'll speak to this in further depth later in the book). Working with elemental spirits, beyond how they might be applied to achieve results, can also help us work with our consciousness and the energetic bodies within us, stabilizing all of them by integrating more fully with the elemental energies.

When I first started practicing elemental magic, I did the exercises in the books I was reading and those exercises helped me connect meaningfully with the first spirits I would ever work with. Those spirits were the elementals and one of the most pivotal experiences I had occurred when I was 18. I had been working with the elemental spirits for almost a year. It was the late winter and I decided to do an experiment. I took out a knife and cut myself, making an offering of my blood to each of the elements, making an offering of my life essence, in return for some of their essence. They agreed to the offer and we exchanged essences. It was one of the most powerful experiences of my life, because it taught me something about the work I could do with the elements. What it taught me was that the elements could be worked with in a way that went beyond the prescriptive boundaries of the books I was reading and that doing so could open me to a different perspective than what was available in those books.

In choosing to make this connection with the elemental spirits, what I really chose was to take on a different perspective of the world, because what the elementals gave me was more than just their essence or a deeper connection to the elemental planes and energies. They gave me a view of the spirits and the world and the elemental forces that I might otherwise not have had. All I needed to do was give them something of equal value. This might seem like an easy thing to do, but it wasn't, because it fundamentally required that I alter my perspective of the world and how I experience life, and this has been an ongoing process as such things ought to be, but more often than not...aren't. We'll come back to this further in the book.

Exercise

What is your history and experience with the elements? What have they taught you about magic, yourself, life in general, and whatever else seems relevant to you? What kind of elemental magic working have you done and how have you worked with the elemental spirits?

Share your answers in the magical experiments Facebook group #WWES.

The difference between nature spirits and elementals

To understand elementals and elemental energies, we must take a moment and distinguish them from nature spirits, because there can be a tendency to conflate the two together. The reason for this is understandable because nature spirits are closely connected to elemental spirits, but there is a distinct difference. Elementals are focused on the primal manifestation of the elements, creating the building blocks of life, while nature spirits tend to the life that is and are an extension and expression of that life. In a later book, I will explore how to work with nature spirits, but focusing on that topic in this book continues the erroneous conflation of the nature spirits with the elementals, which doesn't serve us in any useful way. While

I've summarized the difference between nature spirits and elementals above, let's also consider some other perspectives so that we have a well-rounded understanding of why such a distinction can be useful and important to make:

> There is often confusion over the differences between the elementals and the nature spirits...Most people link them together as either nature spirits or as elementals, but there is a difference. They are all of the same hierarchy (angelic), but they serve different functions at different levels. Those of the nature spirit level are more likely to display 'personality' and the elementals have more of a 'characteristic'...Elementals are the building blocks of nature. They are close to being true energy and consciousness. When we are in contact with them they will stimulate strong responses in us. Learning to work with the elementals is a way of attuning to all of the energies and beings of nature. (Andrews 1993a, Pp. 152-3).

While the concept of a hierarchy is a bit dubious because of what is implied and how it is used to categorize spirits (or anything else), it is worthwhile to note that certain types of spirits seem to show more personality than others. The ones who show less personality, elementals and angels, tend to be more function focused. They are performing very specific functions and those functions seem to be creation based. In contrast the spirits that show more personality such as nature spirits and demons seem to do so because the nature of their work is less function based and more based around interaction, both with humans, and with other aspects of material life. For example, while nature spirits do interact with humans, they also interact with plants, animals, and other aspects of nature and these all require some level of personality that goes beyond a function based perspective. At the same time, what we must acknowledge is that such categorizations of personality and function and hierarchy are human based categorizations, conveniently created by us as a way of understanding the spirits. There's nothing wrong with doing this, but we must acknowledge that such categorizations have an implicit flaw, namely the illusion that they are accurate, when in fact they may not be. Nonetheless, until we can prove one way or another that the categorizations are incorrect, they can still be useful and help us create a taxonomy of the spirits we work with. A different perspective on the role of nature spirits is:

> The term 'nature spirit', or deva, encompasses a wide range of supersensible beings inhabiting the astral-etheric field of the Earth. They assist the angelic hierarchies in the unfolding creation process on Earth, and they assume the guardianship of all physical form. As a general rule, 'nature spirit' is the term used to denote an overarching spirit, or guardian spirit, whose purpose is to oversee a legion of elementals in a specific object or location...Nature spirits mediate the cosmic forces raining in from above and the telluric forces working from below. They are also responsible for preserving the memory of a location from its inner-world and terrestrial-forming activity of the ancient past to the more recent human history residing within (Raven 2012 P. 47).

In this case, the author makes the assumption that the nature spirits oversee the elementals. In my experience, this doesn't hold true and it illustrates the weakness in such categorizations as I mentioned above. The elementals and nature spirits seem to perform distinct roles, but I've never found that the nature spirits have dominion over the elementals. They may sometimes work together, but they also may work on different activities that don't necessarily intersect with each other. I find it interesting and relevant that the author notes that nature spirits mediate the cosmic and telluric forces and in my experience this seems to be true, because in part what they do is bring balance to those energies in the life that they work with. One of the things that nature spirits can teach us is how to do that same mediation, but that topic is for another book.

A final way to understand the difference between elementals and nature spirits involves exploring the distinct differences between nature spirits and elementals: "Another important distinction is that nature spirits and spirits of place often are partly composed of organic life force or are intimately enmeshed with pranic forces. In the case of nature devas, they are general tutelary spirits who guide, govern, or are the spiritual nexus for particular plants, animals, expressions of Elements in nature and so on" (Dominguez JR 2021). In contrast elemental spirits are primal forces, not rooted to a specific place, but rather embedded within everything as part of the weave of creation. They are part of us, and part of everything else, and as a result we can work with them differently than how we would work with a nature spirit or other types of spirits.

How do we connect with Elemental Spirits?

We connect with elemental spirits through the obvious mechanisms of magic, but more importantly we connect with them by feeling them. What I mean by that isn't that we connect with them on the basis of emotions, but rather the more nuanced understanding of feeling. Elementals, in my experience, are beings of movement. *They move us, even as we move them.* We will come back to this theme, but this is something worth meditating on now, as you continue to read this book. Your emotions are one form of feeling and can be useful as a means of connecting with the elemental spirits, but you can also develop your psychic and physical senses to help you with the connection you make with the elementals.

One useful exercise you can do involves learning to touch the elemental energies. For example, you can and do touch air all the time. Put your hand up and slowly move it through the air. What do you notice when you touch the air? What do you notice about how the air touches you? Close your eyes and give yourself over to the sensation of connecting with the air, allowing it to flow around you and move you. If you feel moved to get up, then get up and move, allowing the air energy to work through you (Gray 1980). Take a deep breath and focus on the inhalation and exhalation of breath. What do you notice about how air moves you through the act of breathing? When you connect with an element in this way it teaches you how to open yourself to being moved by it, which is what you initially need to learn how to do, if you truly want to connect with a given element or the spirits that represent it. Once you've learned how to be moved by an element, you can then learn to move with the element and influence that elemental energy.

When you want to work with water, you can take this approach through swimming (in a lake, river, or ocean is preferable, but even a swimming pool will teach you something about the movements of water) or through putting your hand in water. Alternately, focus on the act of taking a drink, because when you drink water you tap into the primal energy of the element of water, and you can feel it's essence move through your body, as well as recognize how essential it is to life. Once you've had this experience with water, translate that into a dance where you express the flow of that specific element through the movements of your body. The use of dance, with all of the elements, allows you to embody the connection you have with the elements, turning your conceptual awareness into embodied experience that fully allows you to take in the elemental energy and then mediate and express it both inward, to your consciousness, and outward to the world around you.

When you want to work with earth, take a walk and make a point to the touch the ground. Dig your fingers into the ground and gently pull on the soil, feeling it and how it permeates your being. Lay down on the ground and allow yourself to feel the terrain, and the way it feels. Touch some stones and feel their strength. Walk barefoot in the grass and let your toes dig into the ground, feeling the earth and connecting with the elemental energies. What do you notice when you connect with earth elemental energy? How does it move you and move through you? In a very real sense, what you are connecting with is the experience of earth that we don't notice and yet is omnipresent in our lives: the subtle movements of the earth that occur in our lives every day.

When you want to work with fire, light a candle or get access to a fire and stare into the flames. Put your hands near the flames to feel the heat. What do you see when you stare into the flames? How does the heat of the fire stir you? Get up and allow yourself to turn those experiences into a dance that embodies the flame and how it moves through you. How does the fire move you and through you? What you are connecting with is the primal force of creativity and destruction, which can manifest great potential, but also bring that potential an end.

When you want to work with spirit, with the quintessence, open yourself to the subtle currents of energy within you and pay attention to how they connect you to the world around you. Spirit is in all things, part of all things, even as it taps us into the potential and imagination that inspires us to turn our thoughts into reality and the spirit itself into manifestation. Commune with spirit and then move into dance. How does spirit move you and flow through you? How do you take the essence of all things and nothing and allow it to inspire your magical work?

This approach to working with the elements provides you a way to embody the elements and come to understand them on all levels of your being. We never want to trap ourselves in a conceptual understanding of the elements. The conceptual provides a framework of sorts, but true connection and relationship with any spiritual force requires us to move past concept into embodied experience and this can only occur when we take actions that allow us to truly experience what we are working with. Doing the exercise I've shared above may seem like a simple activity, but it nonetheless can provide you profound insights into the nature of elementals and the elements, and help you either begin your relationship with them or strengthen the existing ones you have.

Exercise

In some form or manner, whether through dance, like I shared above, or through some movement of your own, connect with the elements. How do the elements move you physically, emotionally, intellectually and spiritually? What does the experience of movement teach you about the elements and you relationship with them?

Share your answers in the magical experiments facebook group #WWES.

Pore Breathing and Elemental Spirits

One of the other ways that you can connect with elemental spirits is through your breathing. In chapter 3, I'll present the Eastern perspective on this practice, but for the purposes of this chapter we're staying rooted in Western magical practices. Franz Bardon shares such a practice in his book *Initiation into Hermetics*, which he describes as pore breathing. It's important to note that the techniques he shares are based on Eastern pranayamic practices. Nonetheless, they've been adopted to specifically focus on the western elements. What you do is breath a specific elemental energy into your lungs and through the pores of your skin (Bardon 2001). Your skin, being porous, takes in oxygen and you can utilize your skin to draw in breath and elemental energies through the pores. With Bardon's technique you accumulate the elemental energy in your body, in a specific organ, if you're drawing on the elemental energies for health reasons, or to direct the elemental energies for magical purposes. The essential idea is that you draw the elemental energies in and when you've accumulated enough of those energies you release and direct them through your body and into the world around you.

As an example of how this works, take your right forefinger. Pick an element and start breathing in and out, accumulating the elemental energy into that finger. Pay close attention to the feeling or experience of the elemental energy in your finger. If you choose fire you will likely a sense of heat or warmth, whereas with earth it may feel dense and heavy. Keep in mind that your experience may differ and that ultimately it is reflective of your relationship with the elements. Now you have this energy in your finger. Think of how you might direct or apply it, either to the world around you or to yourself. Then let go of the accumulated energy and allow it to flow through your body or to the world around you.

I've found Bardon's technique to be useful as a way for mediating elemental energies. I've melded his technique with Taoist qi gong practices in order to help me deepen the relationship I have with elemental spirits. It can also be used to work with spirits in general, as a means of mediating the essence of a given spirit (Ellwood 2020). When I'm doing practical magic and want to apply elemental energies to the mix, I'll draw on the elemental essence of whichever element I want to work with and then direct it into the magical working. For instance, if I'm doing a magical painting and I want to apply the element of air to the painting, I would use pore breathing to accumulate the air element into my painting hand and then during the act of painting release the accumulated elemental energy into the painting. Using Bardon's techniques can be a good way to learn how to work with elemental energies on a practical level and learn how to apply them to your magical workings and the world around you.

Exercise

Try out the pore breathing. Hold up a finger or your hand and as you breathe in, draw in elemental energy into your hand and finger. When you breathe out let it go. Try this same exercise with other parts of your body. How does the elemental energy feel when you bring it into your body and then release it?

Next try this same exercise, but use it during a ritual, drawing elemental energy into your body and then directing it toward a result or toward the working you are doing? How does this elemental energy effect the ritual? What effect does it have on the result you are seeking to achieve?

Share your answers in the magical experiments facebook group #WWES.

How to use sound to connect with elemental spirits

One of the other ways that we can connect with elemental spirits is through the use of sound, specifically the vowel sounds. In the English language, there are five vowels: A, E, I, O, U. In other languages, there are typically more vowel sounds, but for the purposes of this book, those five sounds are convenient because of how they can be mapped to the five classic elements and used as a way to call them in. In one of my spiritual lineages, the fire temple tradition, we use the five vowel sounds to call to the elements, and bring them in to the sphere of art so we can work with them, but also so we can bring the space we are in, into a place of stillness and reverie. Different spiritual traditions will have distinct associations with the vowels and the elements, but none of them are absolutely right or wrong. If anything, the differences in correspondences illustrates how arbitrary correspondences can be.

For example, Ted Andrews has made the following associations between the elements. A = Ether, Fire = I, E = Air, O = Water, and U = Earth (Andrews 1993a). In contrast, RJ Stewart's correspondences are E = Air, I = Fire, O = Water, E = Earth and U = Ether (Stewart 1990, Stewart 1997). And these are just two authors sharing their different perspectives on the elemental energies and the sounds that are mapped to them. If we were to read all the books out that are available on elemental spirits, and look at the specific associations between vowels and the elementals, we'll find some variations. This is useful to know because it allows us to see that there's no set in stone approach to working with the spirits. You can come up with your own correspondences, though you will want to work those correspondences and make sure you understand why those correspondences are in place. Simply choosing to map an element to a vowel sound (or any other correspondence) without doing the work won't make for much of a correspondence or connection, but if you take the time to do the work you'll find that such correspondences naturally fall into place.

In my case, I have taken on Stewart's correspondences, but I have made them my own through the work I've done with them. I will do a vowel chant as a way of fully calling in the elemental spirits. The associations I've made with the vowels allow me to use sound to connect with the elements. When I use sound to call in the elements, I focus on the vibration of the sound. Try this as an exercise. Say the letter A. Now sing the letter A. Now vibrate the letter A. When you say the letter, its just a sound, short and to the point. When you sing it, you bring more of yourself into the sound, because singing requires a bit more effort than just saying something. When you vibrate the sound, which is singing, but more than just singing, you are fully connecting to the energy you are calling forth. When you vibrate sounds you are aligning yourself to the elemental essence that you are associating with the sound. This same principle applies to any kind of spiritual force you want to call on. The act of vibration is an attunement of yourself with the spiritual essence of the beings you are calling to. The resultant connection you have is due to the alignment of yourself to those spiritual forces. The synchronization that results enables you to work with the spirit or other type of spiritual force you have called to.

To illustrate this further, I want you to do the following. In your journal, write down the five classic elements and beside each element write down the sound that you feel goes with that element. Why did you make that specific choice? What it is about that sound that fits with the element you've associated with it? Take a few moments to ponder these questions and then when you are ready, say the sound you've chosen for the element. Next, sing it, and then vibrate it. Allow the sound to go to silence. What do you feel and hear? Are you present with the element? Give yourself a moment to just be and see what you experience.

If you experience nothing, don't be discouraged. Instead, I urge you to continue working with the sound. You are using the sound to introduce yourself to the element you are working with, but don't be surprised if it takes a little bit of time and effort to connect. The elements, in my experience, are receptive, but as with any other spiritual force, they want to see some effort on your part, because that effort speaks to the appreciation you have for the connection you are seeking.

If you experience something, let yourself fully connect with that experience. What is the experience telling/sharing with you about the element? How might you work with that experience and use it to further embody the connection you have with the element? Write down the experience. Then vocalize the sound again and lean into the experience it creates. This sound is one of the ways you can call the elements into your life. You can even combine the sound with the breathing practices shared above. Take in a breath, accumulating the elemental energy you want to work with. Exhale and vocalize the sound you associate with the element, either projecting the element to the world around you, or toward yourself, or some combination thereof. Create a rhythm of sound and breath. Breathe in, drawing the element in, and then vocalize out, expressing it outward. How does this rhythm, slow or fast, help you connect and mediate the element? What do you notice as a result of doing this exercise?

What you are learning to do here, provided you are doing the exercises, is twofold. You are developing an understanding of how correspondences are genuinely developed. It's simply not a matter of slapping a label on a spiritual force and saying, "Welp there it is!" If anything a correspondence is developed because of the work you are doing to experience and develop a relationship that matches the element (in this case) with the sound you've chosen to associate with it. But consider as well that the element HAS chosen that sound to associate WITH you. Correspondences go both ways, but we often only focus on the fact that we're building a correspondence to help us mediate and understand the forces we work with. Yet, if we consider that the correspondence being built goes both ways, it helps us recognize that fundamentally we are all spiritual forces calling to each other and helping each other. Yes, you are a spiritual force, in and of yourself, and you become a correspondence for the spirits you work with. This is the true nature of the relationship you are forming.

The second thing you are learning is how to use the natural resources available to you, in the form of your body, to help you connect with the spirits you want to work with. Yes, you can associate external tools and candles and other various forms of artifacts with spiritual forces. But your voice is a primal mechanism of connection, a potent tool that enables you to call to the spirits and bring forth a connection that is invoked and evoked each time you purposely use your voice to call to the spirits. This is a powerful realization to have because it demonstrates that you are the single most important tool/resource that you bring to your magical work. This doesn't mean you replace your tools or throw them out, but rather that you recognize that you form the foundation of all the spiritual work you do.

Ritual

Using the sounds you have chosen to associate with the given elements, you are going to construct a simple chant/call that can be used to bring the elemental energies into your space. You can do this several ways.

The first way is to simple vocalize the elemental sound in the appropriate that you associate with the element. For example, if I associate E with Air and associate Air with the East, then I would vocalize E while standing in the eastern quarter to invite in the element of air. Do this in each quarter and in the center vocalize the sound for the quintessence.

The second way is a variation, and might be useful if you find you need a little more formality in your work. In each quarter simply state,

"In the direction, I call this elemental power to come forth", and then vocalize the appropriate elemental sound.

This is a simple ritual, but its designed to illustrate the power of sound and how sound can be used to both prepare a ritual space and call forth the spirits associated with the sound. The correspondence you build with the sound is your own, but it provides an effective way to connect with the 5 classic elements without having to use anything else other than your voice.

Magical Tools, the Quarters, and Elementals

Since we're on the topic of correspondences, let us consider some other ways that correspondences can be developed with the elements. Two of the obvious ways are through the cardinal directions of East, South, West, North, and Center, and through the magical tools that we associated with a given direction. Again what I've found is that the association of a given element with a direction and/or magical tool is somewhat of an arbitrary experience. One spiritual tradition might association the element of air with the east, while another associates it with the north. As always, what truly matters is that you develop these correspondences from a place of informed awareness and experience, which allows you to meaningfully connect with the elemental spirits. Likewise a given magical tool ought to be drawn upon or utilized because it represents something specific to your experience with the element you are working with, as opposed to because someone wrote about it in a book or told you that was the way things had to be done. Of course there is value in partaking in the knowledge shared by others, but knowledge only really becomes meaningful when you translate it into experiences that help you reach a state of connection with the forces that you are associating with a given direction and magical tool.

In the spiritual lineage I am part of, I have changed the correspondences with the elements a bit, because I felt that the original correspondences didn't quite match up in a way that spoke to me. Here's the original correspondences: Air/East/Sword, Fire/South/

Rod, West/Water/Chalice, Earth/North/Shield. The center, quintessence was implied, but not signified. I made quite a few changes, based on careful research as well as through work with the appropriate spirits. I didn't change the directions that I mapped the elements to, but I did change the tools and I added a couple other tools. Here's what my correspondences look like: Air/East/Arrow, Fire/South/Rod, West/Water/Chalice, Earth/North/Spade, followed by Underworld/Past/Cube, Cosmos/Future/Crown, and (Center) Quintessence/Present/Cord. I added the last three because I didn't want to just work with a two dimensional representation of the directions and because in my research and work I found that something essential was filled in, when I included directions and magical tools for above, below and the center. I changed some of the tools, getting rid of the more martial aspects in favor of tools that felt more in line with my own experiences with the spiritual tradition.

If you've mapped the elements to specific directions and tools, think back to why you made the associations you made. What helped you come to those decisions? What experiences did you have that confirmed and validated the associations you made with a given tool/direction? No answer is wrong, but it's worth visiting these questions, either from a place of experience, where you have an established relationship with the elemental spirits, or from a place of just starting out and considering how you will make the connections you seek to make with the elemental spirits. As with what you did with the sounds, write down the element, the direction and the magical tool and consider the relationship between all three (and for that matter the vowel sound). How does the direction and tool help you connect with the elemental spirit? Remember as well that the elements are present in all tools, all directions, and all sounds. The choice to use a specific direction, tool, and sound and map it to an element is a personal choice of convenience. It helps you establish a relationship and that should be respected, but it can also become a crutch and as such should always be reviewed and subject to revision, based on the ongoing experiences you have with the elementals.

Ritual

Do another ritual where you call the elemental spirits, but this time include the magical tools that you associate with those elements. Whatever tools you incorporate don't necessarily need a physical representation, though that can be useful. Nonetheless they should be something that represents the connection to the elements and makes sense to you. You may or may not find that the tools are essential to the magical work you do. Pay close attention to the experiences you have, so that you can use them to help you connect meaningfully with the spirits.

Archangels and Elemental Spirits

Let's add one more layer to the correspondence list we're developing with the elemental spirits. The four elements of air, fire, water, and earth have archangels associated with them. From what I can tell with my own research these archangels seem to consistently be applied to the elements, unless of course you're working with a spiritual lineage that doesn't work with the elemental spirits. In such a case, you can likely find appropriate spirits that fit the roles, or maybe even go without those spirits. I know that some magicians will have a kneejerk reaction to working with archangels, because of the association with Christianity, but what should be remembered is that the archangels (and angels) aren't strictly part of Christian mythos and more importantly for our purposes, they are beings that can be worked with, who have some influence on the elemental spirits associated with them. At the same time, what should also be remembered is that each archangel has access to the elemental powers equally, so while a given archangel maybe associated with a specific element, you could also work with that archangel in the context of another element.

The archangel Raphael is associated with air, the archangel Michael is associated with fire, the archangel Gabriel is associated with water, and the archangel Auriel is associated with earth. What about quintessence? I associate the archangel Suvuviel with quintessence, both because of the cord and how the cord is used to wrap everything up and because of how Suvuviel is present in all things, much like how spirit or quintessence is present in all things.

You don't have to work with the archangels in order to work with elemental spirits, but I include them here because it's worth noting the association. If you do choose to work with the archangels, I do find that it provides another level of depth with the work you do with the elemental spirits, because of how the elements and archangels are associated with each other. What working with the given archangel associated with an element provides you is a spiritual authority you can draw on as needed, because that authority is mediated from the archangel.

How do you contact an archangel? You can look up the symbol associated with the archangel and use that symbol and the invocation of the name to call the archangel. Alternately you can do something along the lines of what I've done where you either memorize chants (and all the associations built into those chant) and then use the vocalization of the chant to call the archangel, or you develop your own chants.

Ritual

Integrate the archangels into your elemental magical workings, using either the symbol/call associated with the archangel or memorizing an existing chant, or coming up with one of your own that you memorize. This will take some work and dedication on your part, especially if you opt for the latter choices, but it will also help you build a stronger connection with the archangels as well as the elemental spirits, when you create your ritual and when you do work with elemental magic.

Sample calls:

Hail Raphael, archangel of the East and the element of Air, I call on you to bring inspiration and instruction for this work

Hail Michael, archangel of the South and the element of Fire, I call on you to bring initiation and illumination for this work

Hail Gabriel, archangel of the West and the element of Water, I call on you to bring love and compassion for this work

Hail Auriel, archangel of the North and the element of Earth, I call on you to bring destruction and regeneration for this work.

These are sample calls and they're based off associations I've developed with the archangels, and I've shared them here to give you an idea of how simple it is to come up with a call that you can use to connect with the archangels and bring their energy and presence into your space for elemental magic work.

Working with Elemental Symbols

Finally we come to symbols themselves. While I prefer to work with elemental spirits directly, I do think that the initial process is aided by the use of symbols and/or the anthropomorphization of the elemental spirits. What the symbols provide us is a way to encapsulate the essence of the elementals, but they also act as portals to the elemental planes of existence:

Effective magic uses symbols, placeholders, frameworks, resonant links, and the flexibility of the human psyche to engage with powers that are vaster than humanity, and with those that lie within the Elements themselves are real, but like other great spiritual potencies and presences, only the smallest fraction of their totality can be perceived in the world of dense matter...When you work with the elements, you are accessing some of the primal forces and building blocks that part and parcel of the ongoing process of creation...To work more fully with the Elements, you must exceed the limits of your physical and psychic senses by understanding the process of perception...At the heart of the systems of colors, symbols, magickal tools, correspondences, directional alignments, and so on that are used to call upon the Elements is the assertion that connecting with a small representation of an Element opens a connection to a larger version of the Element (Dominguez 2021 pp 5-7)

What symbols, correspondences, and the anthropomorphization of elemental spirits provide us is a way to tap into that larger elemental energy without getting overwhelmed by it. This is important, especially when you first connect with elemental spirits, because they are primal beings, and because we typically do not have the setup, energetically, to take on too much elemental energy within ourselves. We can gradually build up that connection and take on more of the elemental essence directly, as we learn to connect with the elements through the various methods that are available to us.

When I first started practicing elemental magic, I used the hermetic symbols to connect with the elemental spirits. I also used the anthropomorphized images of the elementals as another way to connect because framing them within a human context helped me understand what I was trying to work with. In my book *Walking With Spirits* I've discussed the problems that arise when you anthropomorphize spirits, but as an initial process for connections with any type of spirits, it can be useful for providing enough context to make sense of the spirits. As you become more familiar with the underlying currents of elemental energies, you can learn to mediate them directly and not rely upon the anthropomorphization or symbols as much or at all (as I will cover later in this book).

If you look below you'll see the symbol for elemental earth and spiritual earth. Each symbol can be used as a door that allows you to connect with elemental energies of earth. You can visualize these symbols, but I think it is more effective to actually create artistic renditions of the symbols, because it simultaneously allows you to imprint the symbol on your consciousness and it creates an external and objective manifestation of the portal that can be worked with beyond the confines of your mind. I recommend first creating the elemental portal. As you draw or paint it, meditate on the symbol and its relationship to the elemental energies of earth. You don't have to use the colors I've used (yellow, green and red), in the picture below. In fact I strongly recommend that when you initially create the art you spend some time focusing on the relationship YOU are developing with the element. You aren't trying to replicate my relationship with the elements. You are forming your own relationship. What colors come to mind for you that represent the elemental earth energy? How do those colors help you connect with earth as an elemental energy?

Next you'll want to create the spiritual earth portal. You'll use this portal in conjunction with the other portal to help you connect with the primal essence of the elemental energy. Again meditate on the symbol and allow whatever colors and associations come to mind to simply steep in your awareness, and then start painting/drawing the spiritual earth symbol. Once you've created both symbols, you'll be able to use them for your work with the element of the earth. Before we get into that work, you'll want to repeat the same process with the symbols for the elemental and spiritual water, elemental and spiritual air, and elemental and spiritual fire. See below for the images I've shared of my art as examples of these elemental portals. Again, I want to stress that you need to create your own symbols and that you don't have to use the colors I've used. Those colors are my personal associations with the elemental and spiritual energies, but yours could be different and they would be equally valid for YOUR practice. Note: If you are reading the paperback and hardback the pictures will be black and white. Blue and green are used with water. Yellow, red and blue with air, and Red and orange with fire.

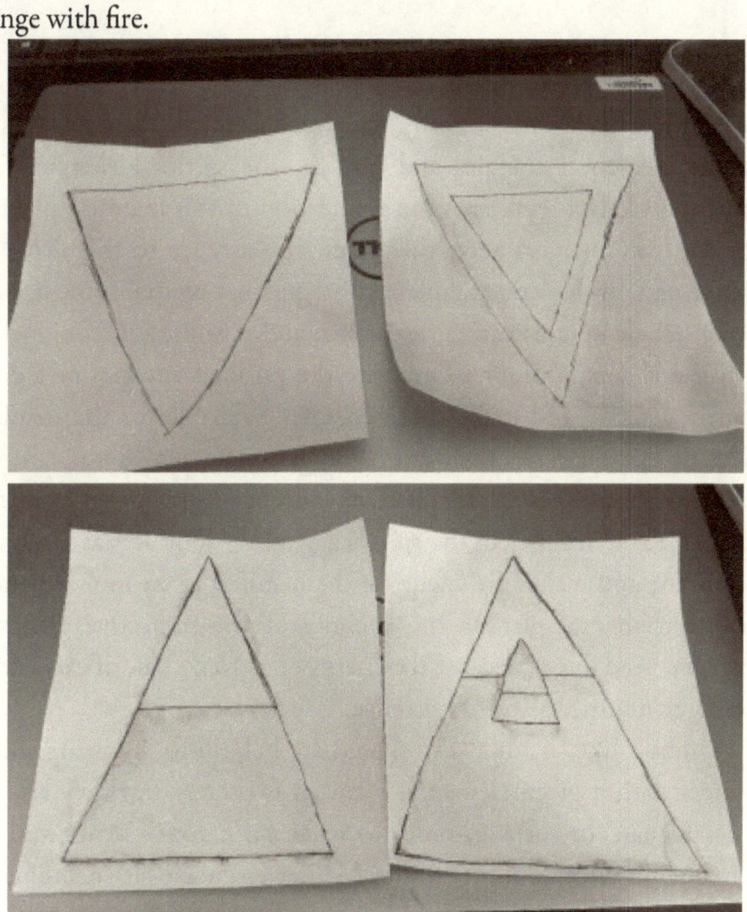

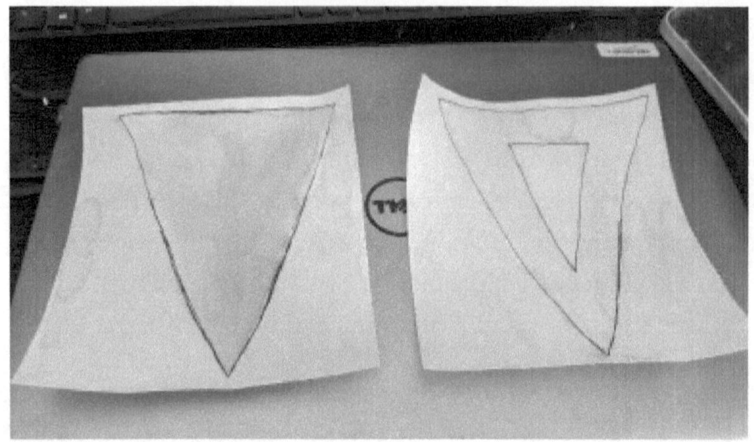

You may be wondering why, with each element, there is a symbol for the elemental energies and one for the spiritual energies. The elemental symbol represents the connection to this manifest plane. It is a doorway that connects this plane of existence to the elemental essence of a given elemental plane. The spiritual symbol is the door to the actual elemental plane of existence and it is used in conjunction with the elemental door to mediate the purified energies of a given elemental plane and make those energies palatable for the manifest plane of existence. At the same time, the elemental door serves to mediate the energies of this plane of existence to the given elemental plane of existence, where the spiritual symbol/door acts as a filter or membrane and makes the energy of the manifest plane more palatable for the elemental planes. The energies of the respective planes of existence need filters, because the energy of a given plane of existence is foreign to another plane of existence.

Symbols like the ones I've shared are helpful for allowing you to connect with a given elemental plane of existence, but they also act as a safeguard of sorts, in order to make both your essence and the elemental essence connect, without either essence overwhelming the other. This is especially useful when you first working with elemental spirits and energies, but what I find most useful about the symbols is that they provide you a way to meaningfully experience the elemental energies and still provide a filter through which you can make sense of that experience.

So now we have our created symbols. How shall we work with them? The first exercise I'm going to recommend is working with the symbols in conjunction with each other. Set up your space so that you have both symbols placed into the environment and then start meditating on the symbols together. What do you notice about your interactions with each symbol as well as the interaction the symbols have with each other? What do you notice about the elemental energies and your energy and how the symbols mediate both? Do this exercise with each set of symbols, paying attention to how those symbols work together and how they work with you. Remember that what you're ultimately working with is a filtered experience of the elemental spirits and energies, but it's also working with you, and what those symbols provide all parties involved is an introduction of sorts that allows you to build the foundation for a deeper relationship.

Another exercise you can do involves setting the symbols up in your physical space. When you do a magical working you can call in the elemental energies through those portals. Admittedly, if you're using some of the other techniques I've described above, you might wonder why you'd want to add the portals into the mix, but I think that the advantage of creating the symbols and using them as portals is that you can set up semi-permanent connections with the elements. The one downside may be how that elemental energy shows up in your life, home, work etc., so I would recommend employing the portals judiciously and knowing when to take them down. Treat them as aids which can provide further access to the elemental energies but know when to use them and apply them.

A final exercise you can do is to use the portals to astrally travel to the elemental planes. Stare into the elemental symbol first and use that to draw you and through to the spiritual door. When you go through the spiritual door you'll visit the elemental plane of existence and be able to interact with the primal essence of the element. The experience will be different from what you know, but it can be a useful experience because it helps you start down the path of directly experiencing and mediating the elemental energies you are working with. You get a sense of how those elemental energies work directly and at the same you don't overwhelm your physical body with them.

Exercise

Take the elemental portals you've created and meditate on them. Meditate first on the elemental symbol and then the spiritual symbol. When you have both symbols imprinted in your awareness, go on an astral journey where you walk through the elemental door to the spiritual door, in order to connect with the elements on their native plane of existence. What happens when you connect with the elemental spirits in this way? What do you learn about the elements when you connect with them on their plane of existence?

Next do a ritual where you evoke the elements using the portals you've created. What do you notice when you work with the elements using the portals? Is it easier or harder to connect with them? How might you apply the portals to your magical work in general?

Share your answers in the magical experiments facebook group #WWES.

Anthropomorphic Elementals

Since we're talking about the symbolism of the western elements, let's explore the anthropomorphic version of those symbols. The anthropomorphic version of elements is essentially a symbolic connection to the spirits which provides a "human" appearance or equivalent that makes it easier for us to interact with the elemental spirits. Earth elementals typically take on the form of gnomes, while water elementals take on the form of undines (nymphs). Air elementals take on the forms of sylphs (winged faeries), while fire elementals take on the form of salamanders, but are these forms the actual nature of the elementals? No. They are precisely what I've said: they are forms taken on by the elemental spirits in order to interact with us, in a way that is filtered toward our preferences and mental sanity. Any spirit, elemental or otherwise, typically takes on an anthropomorphic form because it is the easiest and most convenient way to interact with humans, but it always comes at the cost of a translation issue: We are still experiencing those elemental spirits (or other types of spirits) through a symbolic lens that makes it easier for us to wrap our heads around how to work with those spirits, but makes it harder for us to truly experience them (Abram 1996, Abram 2010, Ellwood 2020). When you first connect with elemental spirits, working with them in anthropomorphic body makes sense. It helps you connect with them and make sense of them.

You can work with elemental spirits through the physical embodiment of the element. If I want to call forth a gnome, then I'll work with soil and use that to connect with an elemental spirit of earth. If I want to work with an undine then I'll work with water from a river or lake or water collected from rain (use a bowl). If I want to work with an air spirit, then I'll connect with the wind and if I want to connect with an elemental fire spirit, then I can work with the flame of a candle. This may seem overly obvious to work with the physical embodiment of an element, but what we must remember is that the elemental spirits are present in those physical embodiments. When we work with the physical embodiment we can call them forth and ask them to take on a form that allows us to work with them.

Don't expect deep, scintillating conversations with elemental spirits. They are very much focused around the functional roles they work within, but they can teach you a lot about a specific element and how to work with it. They can embody and mediate that elemental energy for you and show you how to apply it to your other magical work and they can perform relatively simple workings for you. I've worked with earth elementals for wealth magic for example, because the earth contains the wealth of the land and minerals, but their notion of wealth is different from ours. Where I've really found it helpful to work with elemental spirits is through healing magic for the body and weather magic (we'll cover this in more depth later in the book). You can also work with modern versions of the classic elements. For example I've used the crew of *Cowboy Bebop* to be standins and representatives of the elemental energies. Using a pop culture version of the elemental spirits can be helpful for interacting with them in a modern context, if that's something you need. I've certainly found that working with pop culture representations of the elements can be useful because it provides you a way to connect with the element using a filter that is meaningful to you. Just remember that regardless of how you anthropomorphize the elements, that anthropomorphization is a filter.

There is one final point I want to make. I mentioned that the anthropomorphic forms of elemental spirits are symbols. That does NOT mean that the spirits themselves are symbols. The forms are symbols because of how they are taken on by the elemental spirits (or any other spirit) as a way to interact with us. Humans rely upon metaphor and symbolism to communicate. It's how we understand the world, and because the spirits want to interact with us and have meaningful connections they will oblige that form of communication by taking on a symbolic representation that makes sense to us and enables communication to happen. What we ought to remember is that there ARE multiple ways to communicate and that each form of communication has its advantages and disadvantages. Meditating on this statement will provide you some useful insights about how to work with spirits in general.

Exercise

Work with the elementals anthropomorphically in the ways I described above. What do you discover about your relationship with the elements as a result of working with them anthropomorphically? Is it easier to connect with them using a traditional form such as a gnome or naiad or is it easier to use a pop culture persona?

Call the elemental spirits to you, using the symbols and chants you have come up with. How do they appear to you? How does this appearance help you connect and make sense of them? What are the benefits of working with elemental spirits in this way?

Share your answers in the magical experiments Facebook group #WWES.

Sharing your Life Essence with Elemental Spirits

Everything I've shared in this chapter, up to now, is material you'll find in other books, presented differently, but nonetheless there in one form or another. I wrote this chapter in this way to give us a foundation to work with. For people who have never done elemental magic or worked with elemental spirits, this chapter and the exercises will easily keep you busy for a couple of months, if not longer. All of the work I've shared above is what I did in my first two years of magical practice. I worked with the five elements extensively because I wanted to understand how to connect with them and become an ally to them. I learned a lot, but at 18 (my second year of practice) I came to a realization that the work I was doing with the elements was hitting a wall. There was something fundamental missing and because it was missing I could only take this work so far. I realized that the communication I had with them was part of the problem. It was too limited and I didn't know how to get past that block. I thought about it for a while, and I came up with the first major experiment of my life, something I hadn't read anywhere in books, and yet something that struck me as necessary for taking the next step with the elemental spirits.

Most teachers of the occult will tell you NOT to do what I'm going to suggest. Certainly if I had a teacher at the time, that teacher would have likely discouraged me. Fortunately I didn't have a teacher. I only had myself and the books I was reading and all the books could show me was both the available knowledge and the gaps surrounding that knowledge. This is how experimentation happens. You learn what you can to the point that you hit a gap and then you find a way to bridge the gap or you turn around and go back to the well-known "safe" territory that will box you in and keep you from truly discovering your limitations. In my case, I chose to bridge the gap and as a result it changed my life and put me on the path I am on now. I wanted to have deeper communication with the elementals. I wanted to tap into the power directly and be able to use it instead of working through intermediaries. I wanted to change the structure of my being in a way that would allow me to access the spirit world more directly. Within me was already the seed of this ability, due to circumstances early in my life, but I didn't know how to tap into that seed either. I needed to water it and I needed to change the fundamental structure of my being.

I came up with a ritual where I made an offer to the elemental spirits. I offered my life essence in exchange for their life essence. Was this risky? Undoubtedly, because what it essentially involves is taking this primal elemental energy and making it a part of your being. This elemental energy is already contained with us in minute forms, as it is contained within everything, but I wanted more at my disposal. The challenges of making such an offer is that if it goes wrong it can fuck your life up. Even the success of it has brought complications to my life, because while my essence is more elemental as a result, it has nonetheless made it harder to relate to other people. I'd do it again in a heartbeat though.

The way the ritual worked is that I developed chants of my own to call up the elemental spirits. In the chant, I made my request that I exchange my essence for their essence. I went to a sufficiently wild place to do this work, specifically I went to Rehmeyer's Hollow, near York, PA. Anyone from that area will know about the legend of Rehmeyer's Hollow. If you've visited the hollow, you also know that the energy of that land is darker, because of how one magician murdered another, and because of how the dying magician cursed the land, binding his spirit to it, so that he would always be there. He's still there to this day and I've encountered his spirit. I got his blessing for the working, before I did it. I knew that the magical energies of that area were amplified and I wanted to use those energies to help me with the elemental connection.

I took a knife with me to the ritual work. I did the work at midnight, calling the quarters with the magical tools and associations I already had. Each elemental appeared and I made my case. I wanted to give them some of my life essence in return for some of their essence. Each of them agreed. I took my knife and I cut my right arm. To this day I still have the scar and it still tingles. To this day I also have a deeper connection and communion with the elemental spirits. I took my blood and I offered it to the earth, putting some on the ground. I felt an exchange of energy move from the earth to me, and from me to the earth. I took some blood and I poured it into the lake water, and I felt an exchange of essence go from the water to me, and from me to the water. I took some blood and I gave it to the flame of a charcoal incense and the flame of a candle, putting it on paper so that it would burn. I felt an exchange of essence, my life going to the flame and the flame entering my life. I took some blood and sprinkled it in the air and I felt the wind enter me, becoming me, even as I gave something of myself to the win. Finally, to the quintessence, spirit, I made a libation of blood and gave up a magical tool that was important to me, representing a spiritual connection. I felt the quintessence enter me even as I gave myself to it.

I drove home, using only one hand to drive, because my right arm was numb and the cut was deep. I roughly dressed the wound when I got home and then I feel asleep and I had strange dreams of the elements mixing with me, becoming me, even as I became part of them. They told me, not in words, but through sensation and experience that I had the requested connection but that with it came spiritual work. They wanted to me to take the work with the elemental energies and evolve it past what was already known and they told me I made myself part of them and belonged to them. To this day, I still have this connection with the elements that runs through me and is primal. It has changed the way I experience emotions, because I am moved more strongly by them. It has changed the way I experience and understand the elements.

Could you do something like this? Certainly you could and I won't discourage you if you want to. I've already spelled out the advantages and disadvantages and presumptively you are old enough to make an informed choice and deal with whatever risks comes with this. The first thing you'll need to do is develop your relationship with the elements. If you haven't worked with them extensively already, this simply will not work, because you don't have an existing relationship to work off of. Once you develop that relationship and the time feels right, you'll want to come up with specific chants for each element and memorize them (or be spontaneous but be VERY specific). These chants describe the relationship you want with the elements, and the connection you want to forge with them. Then you need to find a place that is sufficiently and steeped in elemental energy. You'll need to get the permission of that place and any guardian spirits as well. Once the permission is gotten then you'll also want to either bring appropriate representations of the elements or be near the sources, such as a river or lake in the case of water.

You are making a sacrifice. I want to be very clear about that. You are sacrificing some of your life essence in return for their elemental essence. I can't tell you if that changes your life span or not, because I am still alive. What I can say is that it changes your life. You need to understand that, because it will be a change on a fundamental level. You won't be as connected with other people, but you'll be even more connected to the spirit worlds and that brings complications and obligations, as well as power.

You don't have to use a knife. You can use a lancet. Whatever you use should be sterilized, because you are giving blood. You can choose to give other fluids, but blood is the essence of life for us. It is the transmission of our being and what keeps us alive. I don't think any other fluid will quite establish the connection in the way that blood will, but it's your choice. Make the offering and make the exchange, giving your essence for the essence of the elementals.

Final note: You do NOT need to do this exercise to continue working with this book. What I share through the rest of this book is a result of my choice to make this offering but I've written the material so that you can do that work without making this exchange. You should only make this exchange if you fully understand what you are getting into and can accept the consequences. I've shared it here because otherwise it will never be shared. Most occult teachers would tell you not to do what I've shared here. But magic only evolves if we take risks and make changes to what is known to discover the unknown.

Ritual

When you have worked with each of the classic elements long enough, and you feel sufficiently ready, you can do the following ritual, or a variation of your own form, to create the exchange of elemental essence for life essence. Find a wild place, where the elemental energies run thick and strong. You want to do this working in an area where it is easy to connect with the elemental energies. If there are other spirits in the area, you will want to negotiate with them, ahead of doing this working.

What you will need:

Diabetic Lancets

The elemental portals

A red candle for fire

Water

What you will do:

Set up physical representations of the elements in their respective quarters. You can use earth from the air and call in air, but you'll want a candle for fire and water for the water element. You can also place your portals around each representation of the element, with the spiritual portal being placed outward and the elemental portal being placed inward, and the physical representation of the element being placed in between.

Call in the elements and the archangels using the chants you have come up with. Once all the elements are ready, explain that you want to make an offering of your essence in exchange for their essence. If the elements accept, you use the lancets to draw blood and then place that blood on the physical representation of each element. Do this one at a time and each time after you shed blood, take position before the elemental portal and meditate on the element, drawing in its essence, while also sending out your essence to the spiritual portal. Do this for each of the four elements, making the exchange between your essence and their essence.

Once you have done this go into the center of your circle. You'll call in the quintessence, and make another offering of blood, exchange it for spirit and for the power to connect and direct the elemental essence within you. Once this is done, close up the ritual and note any experiences that stand out to you.

Conclusion

This wraps up our first chapter, in which I've covered the essentials for how to connect with the five classic Western elemental energies. This is a good grounding for beginning work with the elemental spirits, but there is much more to explore, including alternative perspectives on the five elements, as well as exploring an evolutionary approach to working with elemental spirits that goes beyond the 5 elements. In this book I'm sharing the result of 30 years of work with elemental magic. It won't be the end all of my work with elemental energies, but it is, for the moment, a description of what I've been up to for the last thirty years. Now let us continue our walk with the elemental spirits.

Chapter 2: The Eastern Systems of Elemental Magic

In the previous chapter I explored the classic Western system of elemental magic in exhaustive detail. In this chapter, we're going to explore the Eastern systems of elemental magic. I am not an expert on these systems, and coming from the Western culture, I likely bring some biases into my understanding of these systems, but I think that it is important to be thorough in exploring the various types of elemental magic systems that are out there (and that I know of). In pretty much every other book I've read on elemental magic I've never seen an attempt to explore or address the differences and similarities of the Western and Eastern elemental systems of magic, which is quite curious to me. On the one hand, in an age where the words "cultural appropriation" are thrown around when any person dares to wander outside their cultural bailiwick, it makes sense that people might be reluctant to discuss the alternate approaches to elemental magic and working with the elemental spirits. On the other hand, since these Eastern systems of elemental magic and spirits have been shared with us, perhaps it behooves to sincerely open ourselves to exploring these systems and discovering how they might influence our understanding and spiritual work with the elements. I have worked with several of these systems, so my understanding and experience of them, such as it is, is not solely based on a conceptual or theoretical approach taken to them. Nonetheless, I am but one person with my own biases and limitations and I explicitly mention that so that as we embark on this exploration, you do it with the encouragement on my part to explore further on your own if you feel called to do so.

One of the biggest differences that stands out to me, between the classic Western system of elemental magic and the Eastern systems, is that the Eastern systems seem to take an integrated approach to working with the elements and spirits associated with them. What do I mean by an integrated approach? In the Western system of Elemental Magic, the elements are classified and treated as separate things that can be worked with. While there is some acknowledgement that the elements are present in all things, there is still a tendency to work with them explicitly as separate beings, and in a manner that I would consider to be mostly cerebral. In contrast the integrated approach of the Eastern systems also acknowledges that the elements are present in all things AND seeks to work with them in all things. Most notably, the focus of Eastern approaches to elemental magic actively integrates the elements into the way you would work with your body, both in terms of energy circulation, but also the physical embodiment and movement of the element. The Western system never really takes this approach to integration. The closest I've found within the Western system is Pogacnik's work, where he comes up with some different body movement exercises for working with the elements, but I've personally found that the qi gong movements developed by the Taoists perform a similar function, and have the added benefit of being developed over thousands of years.

The integrated approach to working with elemental energies and spirits fits into the experiential embodiment approach we want to apply with spiritual work in general. By tuning into how the elemental energies and spirits interact with the body, we open ourselves up to learning how to communicate with them on an experiential level, instead of expecting them to communicate with us through the typical visualization and oral/literate filters that are applied to spirit contact. My work with Laban's theories on geometrical movement and the various Yoga and Qi Gong techniques that can be found in Eastern systems of practices has enabled me to apply experiential embodiment to my work with the elements, creating a more intimate and fused experience of communication. Pogacnik's techniques could also be used in a similar fashion, because they also focus on creating a similar embodied experience. We will touch on this in further depth, in future chapters, but for the moment let's focus on the Eastern systems of elemental magic and spirit work.

Dzogchen/Tantra/Bon

Each Eastern system of elemental magic has its own version of the elements, which doesn't necessarily mesh with the Western system, even though there are 5 elements in each system. In the case of the Tibetan system which is a fusion of Dzogchen, Tantra, and Bon, we have the following explanation:

> In Tibetan culture, the five elements - earth, water, fire, air, and space - are considered to be the substance of all things and processes...The names of the elements are symbolic. They suggest a description of particular qualities and modes of action by analogy to the familiar elements of the natural environment. As in most cultures, the Tibetan tradition uses the natural elements as fundamental metaphors to describe forces both internal and external...But in the Tibetan tradition the elements are not only understood metaphorically. Rather, the elements in nature concretely represent a subtler and more fundamental discrimination of five aspects of the primordial energy of existence (Rinpoche 2002, P. 1).

While I disagree with the author's notion that other cultural approaches to elemental work is strictly metaphorical, it is worth noting that a distinction is made around working with the elements from a place of appreciation that extends beyond a strictly intellectual exercises. This subtler work is focused around achieving balance with each of the elements, both in the relationship that the elements have with each other and in the relationship the elements have with the practitioner. This balancing of the elements can occur on multiple levels, through practical magic applications designed to get results, to doing divine communion work with the elements. The act of elemental balancing is an ongoing work within the Tibetan system, because there is a fundamental recognition that the elements are always moving and changing in relationship to each other. This is something explicitly explored in Eastern systems of elemental magic, in contrast to the Western system, which tends to treat the elements as relatively static expressions of being. The benefit of the Tibetan approach is that it emphasizes the active relationship that the elements have with each other and encourages the practitioner to work with them, not as separate entities, but rather as part of a holistic approach to the spiritual work that is done in general: "When we understand the inclusiveness of the five elements, we see that everything arises together, nothing is completely separate from anything else and everything is affected by everything else...Applying an understanding of the elements to our experience, we can usefully describe and examine any situation in any dimension...When we experience grosser or subtler levels of the elements, we are actually experiencing grosses and subtler levels of ourselves" (Rinpoche 2002 P. 12). This nuanced approach enables the practitioner to do meaningful internal work around the elements, as well as focused externalized manifestation work (similar to my elemental balancing ritual, which I'll share further in the book), because the overall focus is on developing a balance with the elemental powers, as it plays out within both the internal and external aspects of our lives.

If there is one aspect of this system that is similar to the Western system it is that both systems rely up on symbols and concepts to connect with the elemental powers and spirits: "All of the levels work with symbols and concepts connected to the elemental energies because symbols are how we relate to the energetic processes" (Rinpoche 2002 p. 29). This reliance upon symbolism and concepts does lead to a similar distancing from the elements, but the Tibetan system finds a way around this through the simple acknowledgement and realization that spirits are everywhere. Each rock, stream, tree, etc., has its own spirit and each spirit has its own autonomy and can choose whether to work with us, oppose us, or just do its own thing, separate from us. This approach to spirits is similar to the nature spirits in Western magic, but Dzogchen makes an interesting distinction in that it argues that the spirits are the elements, whereas in Western magic, nature spirits are treated as distinctly different from elemental spirits (Andrews 1993a, Andrews 1993b, Rinpoche 2002).

The four elements of earth, air, fire, and water are treated in a similar way to the Western descriptions of them. The fifth element, space, is different from spirit/quintessence in the West: "Everything arises from space, exists in space, and dissolves into space. In us that sacred element of space manifests as awareness. Experience is what arises in awareness, as the content of awareness...When the space element is balanced in us, there is room in life; whatever arises can be accommodated" (Rinpoche 2002, p.19). While it might be tempting to try and fit the element of Space into Quintessence, I think that there is a very real difference because of how the element of space is treated in Dzogchen. Space is considered the mind and the experiences we have and this isn't quite the same as Quintessence. Space is an inseparable state of awareness and emptiness, and ideally the practitioner comes to an awareness where they become that space, as opposed to whatever arises in that space (Rinpoche 2002). It's a good reminder as well not to force a fit between one system and another, when it comes to what is different.

There are a number of practices that you can do with Dzogchen for elemental work, including elemental energy retrieval and the circulation of elemental energy in your body. One of the best ways to experience elemental energy in your body is to do pranayamic breathing, which is similar to what Franz Bardon writes about in his books. The following exercise can help you with this breathing and being able to connect with elemental energy. It's the nine purification breaths and it's designed to open and clear the energetic channels.

Sit in a comfortable position, either in a chair, with both feet on the ground, or cross legged. Cup your hands together, with your left hand resting on your right hand. Sit up straight, but relaxed. Don't force your back to be tense, and tuck your chin a little. This will straighten your neck. You can keep your eyes open or closed for this particular exercise.

When you breathe in for the first three breaths, you will take your right forefinger and put it against your right nostril, closing it. When you breathe for the first three breaths, you will take your left forefinger and put it against your left nostril, closing it. Try this now. What you may notice is a feeling of clarity as you breathe in and out. What you are doing is stimulating the energetic channels of your body.

For the next three breaths, you will take your left forefinger and put it against your left nostril, closing it, when you breathe in. When you breathe out you will take your right forefinger and put it against your right nostril, closing it. You are doing this alternating process for the next three breaths to further clear out your energetic channels and help you reach a deeper state of relaxation.

For the final three breaths, you will breathe in and out with both nostrils. This will allow you to raise the energy in your body through your head and create a very receptive state of being for working with the elemental energies and spirits (though you can use this practice for working with other spirits as well). You can do this breath work with either short, focused breaths or with longer, deeper breathing, depending on what state of experience you want to cultivate. The shorter breaths call up the energy more quickly and sharpen your focus, but they are more forceful, whereas as longer, deeper breaths create a more relaxed state of being. I use the shorter breathing when I want to call and direct the energy for an external purpose, and I use the deeper breaths when I want to do deeper internal work and energetic circulation of the elements (or any other energy I want to work with).

After you have done the nine breaths, you can continue to breathe through both nostrils and focus on connecting with a specific elemental energy/spirit. You may want to use a setting where the element is represented. For example, if I want to work with water, I might do this breathing by a river, lake, or ocean, or have a bowl of water on hand. With earth, I might find a place with lots of plants and toiled earth to work with. In the case of fire, I might use a candle or sit in an area where there's a lot of sun, and in the case or air, I might find a high place, like a cliff, where I can work with air. In the case of space, you can connect with the night sky or the space in a room. If you can't travel all over the place, you can still work with the elemental energies and spirits, because they are always present around us. Find a place in or near your home that represents that elemental energy. You might find a tree or a bush near your home, or light a candle or work with a bowl of water, or whatever else helps you connect the element you want to work with.

The nine purification breaths is the initial practice you would do to prepare yourself to work with the elemental energies in the case of both elemental energetic retrieval and the circulation of the elemental energies in your body. The Dzogchen technique for elemental energy retrieval is a fairly involved process that involves doing guru meditation, where you call in the Buddha or a teacher, if you have worked with one and then call in the four guests, and do other specific practices to help you with the process of retrieving the elemental energies. I would recommend reading *Healing with Form, Energy, and Light* by Tenzin Wanygal Rinpoche, where he discusses this working in more depth. I haven't included it in this book, because it is a very specific cultural practice, with a fairly elaborate process that really ought to be learned directly from someone who has performed it.

Instead, using the nine purifications breath as a base technique to connect with the elemental energies, I present one method you can use to circulate elemental energies in your body, for the purpose of achieving better balance with those elements. This practice can be done without having a formal background in Dzogchen. It is based around using the western elements, but you can us the Dzogchen elements instead. It draws on the breathing practices shared here, as well as vocalization of the elemental energies to help you connect with and balance the elements within you.

Ritual: Elemental Circulation and Balancing

Once you've done the nine purification breaths, connect with each elemental energy in turn, for nine more breaths, repeating what you did above. As you are doing the breathing with each element, pay close attention to any elemental energy that feels deficient within you. You will want to call that elemental energy to you. To do this what you will do is use the vowel sound you associated with the specific element to help draw that elemental energy into you.

For example, in my system, if I need to retrieve earth elemental energy, I would vocalize the vowel O, which I associate with earth, in order to draw that elemental energy to me and circulate it within my body. I vocalize that vowel until I have gathered enough elemental energy to work with and then what I do is continue breathing and circulate the elemental energy through my body, with the goal being to rebalance that energy. Don't force yourself to hold on to that elemental energy or put more into your body than you can handle. That will only create more of an imbalance. Instead you simply want to breathe in the energy and let it flow through your body.

The elements, in both Dzogchen and Taoism are associated with specific organs, and what you can do is direct the elemental energy to the organ it is matched, because that internal organ will help you regulate the elemental energy. Keep in mind that the organ associations for Dzogchen are different from Taoism (which I'll cover below). In Dzogchen, the element of earth is associated with the spleen, the element of water is associated with the kidneys, the element of fire is associated with the liver, the element of air is associated with the lungs, and the element of space is associated with the heart.

For the purposes of this working, you'll want to match the elemental sounds with the appropriate organ, but keep in mind that this association is arbitrary, based on whatever system you are working with. You will want to feel into this work and pay attention to how your internal organs respond to the elemental energy, to determine if this is correct. If it feels incorrect STOP the breathing and don't go any further, because otherwise you could mess yourself up energetically and it will have detrimental physical health effects as well. I say this with some experience, which I'll share further in the Taoist section.

Again you don't want to draw on too much. For example, if you want balance with fire, you don't want to draw so much fire into your liver that you end up destabilizing yourself. Instead you want to breathe the fire in and circulate it through your body and then stop the circulation when your body feels satisfied. You will do this circulation by breathing in through both nostrils, taking long deep breaths. Don't do fast breathing for the kind of work, because with fast breathing you are forcefully directing the elemental energy and you DO NOT WANT to do that with breathing for the purposes of circulating and rebalancing elemental energies. It will create blockages that could be problematic. You have been warned.

Breathe in deeply and smoothly. As you breathe in, let the elemental energy flow into your body. Don't direct it too much beyond sending it to the appropriate organ, which in and of itself can help you direct the energy. When you breathe out, let the elemental energy flow out of you, taking away any impurities or blockages as it goes out. Continue this practice until you have achieved a state of balance and awareness with the specific element you chose to work with.

You can work with all five elements in a session, but I recommend building up to that process. Initially, just work with one element and get used to feeling how that elemental energy interacts with your body and consciousness. If you can connect with an elemental spirit, pay close attention to the connection and write down any impressions or information you've received from the elemental spirit that can be worked with later.

If you choose to work with the element of space, you'll want to connect with that feeling of spaciousness, allowing it to pervade your being. You could use the sound you associate with quintessence of this element, because even though there are some differences, there are also similarities. I use the sound UOOO for quintessence, and it's a sound that contains all the other elements. In the case of the element of space, in Dzogchen, it also contains the other elements, so it can be worked with in a similar way, but what this element teaches you is how to create and hold space with all of the other elements, and with your awareness, creating an overall balanced state of being.

Conclusion

If you want to learn more about Dzogchen elemental practices, I strongly recommend picking up *Healing with Form, Energy, and Light* by Tenzin Wangyal Rinpoche and /or getting involved in the Dzogchen community. My own interests in these practices has been informed by wanting to have a grounding in how these practices work, but I have opted to focus more on the Western and Taoist practices because they are a better fit for my temperament and focus of my work. That's me though, and I had this realization after having worked with various Dzogchen practices for about four years. I ended up doing less overt elemental magic work. I ended up going too deep into the internal work and didn't find the balance I wanted, as far as the practical aspects of magic went. I suspect part of that could be due to cultural differences, but it could also simply be that these particular elemental practices weren't the right fit for me. As with anything else though, I encourage you to explore and get your own answers, because that's how you develop as a magician.

Hinduism

In Hinduism the five elements are essentially the same as the elements described in Dzogchen, but there is a key difference, which is worth noting. I have not worked within the Hindu system of elemental magic. What I'm sharing here is mainly provided for purposes of being thorough on this particular topic. Just as with Dzogchen, the five elements are earth, water, air, fire and space. The one difference (as far as I know) is that the Hindu system of Ayurveda includes something about the elemental powers that I've never seen in any other system:

> The Three Dosa of Ayurveda themselves condense from the Five Greater Elements. Vata arises from Air and Space, pitta from Fire and Water, and kapha from Water and Earth. The dosas, which are more substantial than prana, but less substantial than the Five Elements, gravitate to the parts of the organism where their originating elements concentrate. The condition of the dosas in a living organism thus directly reflects the condition of the Elements in that body. Though it might seem counter intuitive that the dosas, themselves made from the Elements, are nevertheless less substantial than them, this fact is precisely why the dosas can move the Elements around - each dosas is in a way a 'joint' generated at the point where two of the Five Elements meet and must interact (Svoboda 2013, pp-63-4).

The three Dosa essentially serve as connectors between the elemental powers and a way to manipulate or work with the elemental energies. In Ayurveda, for example, there are specific dietary types of food associated with the Dosa that can be used to work with the elemental energies in the body. I've never come across this approach in other systems of elemental magic and I can't comment on this practice, beyond noting it here, since I have no experience with it, but I mention because it does provide a possible angle for further elemental work, if that is something you want to pursue.

Taoism

Taoist practices have their own unique approach to elemental energies, and the focus of that approach differs quite radically from the Western, Dzogchen or Hindu systems of elemental work, and yet can be usefully integrated into elemental magic work in general, precisely because it is so different. The focus of Taoist elemental practices is on the movement of qi and specifically how that movement can be adapted to the way the elements work. It is less about working with actual elemental energies and/or spirits and more about understanding how to apply the elements to the way energy is moved in the body or in the environment. This is crucial to understand, not only in terms of getting the Taoist elemental system, but also for developing a refined appreciation for internal and external energy work:

> According to Taoist tradition, all matter and human dynamics are comprised of some energetic combination of Earth, Water, Wood, Fire and Metal. Just like electricity, which can take millions of forms depending on its use, elements change to match the energy fields in which they are operating...The elements take different forms according to which of the eight energy bodies they dominate and how they interact with one another on both intrapersonal and interpersonal levels...The five elements are interrelated - there are no distinct boundaries. Fire produces Earth; Earth gives birth to Metal; Metal produces Water through condensation; Water grows Wood; Wood feeds fire...each element influences, bleeds through and melds into the next one...the elements only exist within an intricate relational and energetic matrix with one phase yielding to and encompassing the next in a continuous cycle (Frantzis 2012 pp. 128-29).

In Taoism, the elements are explicitly linked to the internal organs: Earth to spleen, Water to kidneys, Wood to liver, Fire to heart, and Metal to lungs and spine. You might note that this association with the organs is different from the Dzogchen association with the organs, which again demonstrates how arbitrary these associations can be (and why it can be useful to ultimately come up with your associations based off the work you do with the elements).

The way you work with the elemental energies in your body can help you connect with the internal organs and bring some balance to your emotions and overall health. For example, let's say you have too much fire. You'll definitely feel that fire energy in your heart, but also throughout the rest of your body. You can do qi gong that works with the water element to cool down your heart and bring balance to your energetic bodies. One thing to keep in mind, as noted in the above quote is that each of the elements feeds into another element. It's a good idea to learn each element and work with it, in order to learn how to apply them to each other and your physical and energetic bodies. The most important thing to understand about the Taoist approach to the elements is that the overall focus is on the how those elements move in the world and in the body, both when things are in harmony and when they are not in harmony. The Taoist approach emphasizes that the elements are innately part of us and can teach us how to move and interact with world through the elemental energies that are always active and present within us.

In my own qi gong work, I've been gradually working with the elements, learning how to adapt myself to the particular sensation and experience of a given element. The metal element for example is great for working with the intellect because it is sharp and emphasizes clarity of thought and focus. In contrast the wood element focuses more on growth and building up the energy of the body. The water element is restful, dissolving whatever is otherwise occupying your mind and awareness, while also emphasizing rest and recovery. The fire element stirs the emotions up, while also lighting up one's sense of creativity and imagination and the earth element grounds all of it, providing stability and foundation to support everything else. Yet with all of these expressions of the elements there is a sense of movement and change, and no one of them is automatically better than the other, though one may be more prevalent for a person. In the Taoist system, I would fall under the category of the fire element, because of my creativity and emotional fire. Nonetheless I have learned to balance that out with the other elements. The point of working with all the elements in qi gong is to find the necessary internal and external balance between them and yourself so that you can evolve as a person, but also work with the environment around you more conscientiously.

There are different schools of Taoist Qi practices, notably the fire and water school of practices. Both of these schools use many of the same practices, but the way they use them differs depending on the focus of how qi is moved. The fire school focuses on more forceful projection of the elemental energies and relies upon visualizations and the use of vibration for directing the elemental energies, while the water school focuses on more of an embodied experience, where you learn to work with the element in a way that isn't forceful and works more within your limits. I've worked with both schools of practice and my preference is to work with the water school of practice because it is much more natural and there is less of a chance of creating potential energetic and physical health problems. I did have an experience of qi sickness that occurred because of the fire school practices I learned.

My Experience with Qi Sickness

Some years back, I was learning a rather elaborate system of working with the Taoist elements, as well as circulating the stellar and underworld energies through breath. There was a lot of visualization associated with this system, and you had to construct energetic structures that were supposed to help you regulate and direct the energies you were working with. In retrospect, the biggest lesson I learned from this experience that I still apply to ALL of my magical practice is never create energetic structures or do work that is needlessly complex because it can create issues and problems that you didn't need to experience. I am fairly certain that the practices I was learning left key information out and/or that certain precautions were not stated as they should have been. I am NOT including these practices in this book because I do not want you to do anything foolhardy that could harm yourself and I am not convinced that the benefit of these practices outweighs the harm of them.

I did these practices for several months and while initially I didn't note anything unusual, I did find that the visualization practices in particular seemed excessive and took me away from working with the body, even though they were designed for the purposes of regulating and directing qi in the body. Anytime you do a practice that involves your body, it should take you into your body and into the experience of how the qi/energy works with the body. If it takes you away from your body, that's a red flag right there.

A couple months in I started to notice that I felt less energetic and also was starting to get sick. I rarely ever get sick, so when I noticed that I was getting sick more frequently and not feeling like my normal energetic self, I did a check in with myself and realized that the energetic structures I had built and the practices I had learned were making me sick. My qi felt sluggish. I stopped the practices and resumed the water school of qi practices and within a month was back to normal. Fortunately I was already so attuned to my body that I picked up what was happening quickly, but if I hadn't been it could have really messed me up and I have heard other anecdotal stories that indicate that if the fire school practices aren't done correctly, or you aren't energetically built for those practices, they can really mess you up.

I do want to note that any internal energy practice has that potential, including the water school practices. It's best to learn these practices from a teacher, if you can, and if you can't go slow and take your time, really feeling into the experience and noting carefully what the different experiences feel like. If something feels off or incorrect STOP doing the practice! Don't force yourself to do something that doesn't feel right. Your body, energetic and physical, will let you know and you must carefully pay attention, so that you don't mess yourself up. You have been warned.

Water School Breathing Meditation

Breath is the gateway to the body, initially, even though in the end it may not matter as much. We use breath, because we all need to breathe, and because it can create a natural rhythm that we can work with. You breathe in and out every day and you likely don't think about it, unless you're doing an activity where you need to pay attention to the breath, such as meditation, Ultimately, however, you want to get a point where you don't think about the breathing in meditation, and instead simply breathe, focusing on the experience that is occurring.

With Taoist breathing, you breathe in and out through your nose, while touching the tip of your tongue to the roof of your mouth. If you say "la" right now, the tip of your tongue will brush the roof of your mouth and that's where you want it to be while you are doing Taoist breathing. When you breathe in and out, you want to breathe with your diaphragm and you want the sides of your body and your back to expand and contract with the breathing. This will massage your internal organs and help with the circulation of fluids and qi in your body. Put this book down and take a few moments to breathe like this.

When you learn to breathe like this, it can help you with dissolving practices for internal work, which I have covered in my book *Inner Alchemy of Internal Work*. However it can also help you with the circulation of external energies, such as elemental energies. I have even used it to help me commune with spirits, because this kind of breathing technique quiets the mind and opens you to bring more receptive to the spirits.

Ritual: Taoist circulation of the elements through breath

For this working all you need is your breath and to be able to get into a state of mind where you are receptive and focused. Once you are in that you will focus on the qualities of the qi you are circulating with the breathing meditation. Each element has its own distinctive quality which shapes how you work with that qi.

Working with the element of wood is an experience of growing energy. The liver is the organ associated with wood qi and when you want to circulate this type of energy, you can draw on the liver as well as that experience of growth.

Working with the element of metal is an experience of sharp mental clarity. The lungs are the organs associated with metal, as is the spine. When you want to circulate this type of energy, you can draw on the lungs and the feeling of clarity and sharpness of mind.

Working with the element of water is an experience of rest, of settling into things. The kidneys are the organs associated with water. When you want to circulate this type of energy, you can draw on the kidneys and the experience of rest and recover.

Working with the element of fire is an experience of creative and destructive energy. The heart is the organ associated with fire. When you want to circulate this type of energy, you can draw on the heart and the feelings of creativity or destruction.

Working with the element of earth is an experience of balance and harvesting. The spleen is the organ associated with earth. When you want to circulate this type of energy, you can draw on the earth and the feelings of balancing and harvesting.

When you are doing the breathing meditation, you can draw on these distinct elements and the feelings associated with them in order to move your qi. The experience of working with any given element is going to differ from the other elements, because of how you are moving and circulating the qi. This is the important distinction to understand in qi gong work with the elements. The experience of the qi and how you hold presence with it and move it is what provides you the insight for how the elemental powers work.

Get into a relaxed sitting posture, with your left hand cupped into your right hand. Touch the tip of your tongue to the roof of your mouth and start breathing in through your nose and out through your mouth. Give yourself five minutes to just focus on the breathing and get into a relaxed state of being. Once you feel relaxed starting drawing in the qi with your breath. When you breathe in draw it up to the top of your body and when you breathe let it flow down into your body.

As you are breathing, you may feel points of tension. Don't try to force your awareness through those points of tension. Instead simply rest your consciousness on the points of tension. With each breathe, allow your awareness to flow around the point of tension, like water flowing around a rock. If that point of tension dissolves, acknowledge whatever comes up, but continue to breathe and sink your awareness into your body.

Once you are in a deep enough state of altered awareness, you'll want to draw on the element of choice and continue the breathing exercises. When drawing on an element, you want to draw on the movement of the element and allow that movement to transform your experience of the qi. When you draw on the wood element, you will feel the qi growing in you and prompting growth as well in your life. When you draw on the metal element, you'll feel a sense of clarity and focus enter your mind. With water you'll achieve a state of restfulness and with fire a sense of creativity or destruction and with earth there will be a sense of balance. When breathing with the element, allow yourself to feel into the way the element changes the qi. Don't try to force it or fight it, but instead simply open yourself to the experience of the qi and recognize how working with a given element transforms the experience of the qi and how it moves through you.

As you become more proficient with a given element you can work with it to help you enhance your health. For example, if you needed some sense of growth, you could draw on the element of wood while doing breathing meditation to help you cultivate that sense of growth in your life. The same principle applies to the other elements, where you draw on the specific attributes of the element and use that to help you in an area of your life where you need that element or use it to enhance your physical, emotional, mental, and spiritual health. To do this you simply draw on the element you want to work with, connecting with the way it changes your qi and then cultivate the elemental qi within you.

Standing Qi Gong Practices

One of the best ways to experience the movement of qi, whether you're working with the elements or not, is through standing qi gong practices. With standing practice, you feel the upward and downward flow of the qi, as well as the fluids of the body and this helps you tune into the qi within you and in the environment around you.

You'll, obviously, want to stand when you do standing qi gong. Your feet should be parallel to each other, as if they were train tracks. You don't want to stand like a tall, stiff board. Instead you want to stand in a way that is flexible and allows you to relax into the standing posture you are in. When you stand, you want to "sit" slightly, sinking your hips and butt just a little bit so that your knees bend slightly. Your back should be straight, with your chin tucked slightly, so your neck also straightens. Your arms should be at your side, turned or twisted slightly so that your palms face behind you.

When you are doing standing qi gong your tongue will touch the roof of your mouth and you'll breathe in and out through your nose. You can rock your feet slightly so that when you breathe in, you sink on your heel and when you breathe out you move your weight slightly so that you end up being on the ball of your foot, which is also known as the bubbling well. This rocking sensation shouldn't be forced, but instead should be a slight sensation that you feel as you stand. It will help with the raising and lowering of the qi.

When you stand, you'll do the breathing meditation, and when you connect with the qi, you'll sink it into your body, allowing it to dissolve any blockages that you encounter, but once again don't force it. You simply want to sink your awareness in your body and allow it flow around whatever it encounters gradually dissolving it.

As you breathe, while standing, you may also feel a sensation of qi rising in your body. This will especially begin to happen as you begin the rocking sensation I described above. It's useful for you to feel this and recognize that qi and the fluids of your body don't just go down, but also up, and for that matter to the sides. The experience of this sensation can help you become attuned to the sensitivities of the qi and to the realities of your body.

Once you get used to the standing exercise, it can be helpful to integrate the elements into the standing qi gong. Once again what you'll want to do is draw on the specific elemental attributes that are associated with the elements. Connecting with the element of wood requires that you draw on the experience of growth, while drawing on the element of metal draws on the experience of mental clarity and so on and so forth with each of the other elements. One thing you will want to pay attention to is how your body physical responds to the elemental energy. For example, when I work with the wood element, my body becomes suppler and I work with the ligaments more, whereas with the metal element the sensation is more rigid and I work more with the tendons of the body.

What I've described here is a fairly basic approach to standing qi gong. I recommend doing standing qi gong for at least twenty minutes a day so that you can get an experience of it that helps you appreciate how your body settles into the experience of standing. The unfortunate reality of writing a book on a topic such as qi gong practices is that text, even with illustrations, will never fully capture the experience of doing the practice. You can do everything I've shared here and it will be helpful to you, but there are subtleties that can't be fully conveyed or experienced, save through in-person training, or at the very least videos where you can watch what someone else is doing and get a sense as to what you should be doing. This is one of the reasons I'm not touching on qi gong exercises, where you move, in this book. Instead I would recommend that you check energyarts.com, which is the website for Bruce Frantzis. He is a genuine Taoist master and offers in person and livestream training which will help you take what I've shared much further and allow you to fully appreciate the subtleties of this work.

Conclusion

What I've attempted to do in this chapter is give you an overview of the Eastern systems of elemental work. This is just an overview, but I hope that it gives you some insights into other systems of elemental magic and spiritual work, both in comparison and contrast to the Western system that we're familiar with. I would urge you to check out the resources in the bibliography to learn more about these systems and do your own research and practice as well, so that you can determine if and where these practices fit into your life. I also want to note that all of these practices have been intentionally shared with the West, so choosing to learn them is not an act of cultural appropriation. Now let us return to the Western system of elemental magic, but introduce some new elements to it!

Chapter 3: An Expanded Definition of what Elementals are

I want to circle back to the question what are the elements. Are there only the 5 classic western elements, or is there more to it than just the five we know of? In fact, there is, if we simply look at other cultures, which have their own version of the five elements, as we've explored in the previous chapter. So there are different variations of the five classic elements and how we work with those variations can also differ from how we would work with the 5 classic Western elements. Yet even with those variations, I think that there is still something profound being missed out on when it comes to elemental magic. The question is: What's missing and where do we find it?

For example, do we turn to the periodic table of elements and start working with them as elements? They fit the Western definition of being the building blocks of creation. Without the elements of the periodic table, known and unknown, we wouldn't exist and this material reality would be different, so we could certainly work with the scientific elements. In fact a great example of such work can be found in the Elemental Hexagon deck developed by Calyxa Omphalos. Yet I think even working with the elements of the periodic table, while making for a very fun experiment with elemental magic doesn't fully address the question that I've asked above. I think the answer to my question lies in redefining what the elements are and how they show up in our lives.

My definition for the elements is different from the classic Western definition. The classic Western definition treats the elements as the building blocks of life, but an essential aspect of elemental energy and being is ignored by that definition. There is one thing the elements have in common: Movement. The elemental spirits and the elements themselves move us and the world and in turn are moved by us and the world. Meditate on that statement and consider that perhaps the nature of an element isn't just to be a building block, but to tap into something primal and essential that moves through all of us in some form or manner. When we consider this, it also opens the door to consider that there may be many more types of elemental energies and spirits than we have previously considered. Why limit ourselves to 5 elements, when perhaps there are many more that can be worked with?

My experience with elemental magic and spirits is that there are a lot more elemental types and energies than is typically considered in occult thought and practice. Yet what I've also noticed is that any attempt to explore this taxonomy of elements is ultimately roped back into the classic 5 elements. In order for me to establish that my definition could be valid I want to explore in further depth the origins and contemporary perspectives of the 5 classic western elements, and at the same time explore what is problematic about those perspectives.

The Origins of the 5 classic Western Elements

The origins of the classic Western elements occurred in ancient Greece. Empedocles was the first to write about the elements, followed by Plato and Aristotle, but since Greece was an oral culture first, the elements were likely being discussed and worked with before they were written about (Barrabbas 2021, Tyson 2020, Dominguez 2021). As was shared in the first chapter, the understanding of the elements is that they are present in all things, to one degree or another, albeit with one element typically providing the dominant nature. For example, a person who is fiery by nature would have all the other elements of earth, water, and air present within them, but would tend to have more fire than the rest, which could be used to explain their behavior but also their health. The 4 humors in health come from this elemental model as it is applied to us and it is also used as a way to describe behavioral aspects. In the first chapter what you essentially did (if you did the exercises) is create a correspondence chart. The classic elements are a very convenient and simple system for developing correspondences and mapping attributes and behaviors, but what ought to be remembered is that within that capacity the elements become metaphors that help categorize and describe specific behaviors, symbols, etc. Nonetheless they can also become a crutch of sorts, because those same behaviors and attributes are also used to produce a filtered understanding of the elements.

The Anthropomophization of the Elements

Should we then do away with correspondences systems?

Not at all! They serve very useful purposes and can help us develop in-depth relationships with the spirits we work with, as well as show us how to work with the spirits and apply their skills and experience to the situations where we need their help. Correspondences have a very useful role in occultism. At the same time we shouldn't make the mistake of thinking of them as the end all be all, when it comes to developing relationships with spirits, or with other aspects of spiritual powers we work with. Correspondences help us map out the territory, but we must remember the cliché that the map isn't the territory. We also need to recognize that a fundamental purposes of correspondences can actually take way from the purity of connection we can have with spirits: "Humans have tried to classify the numerous kinds of beings of nature. Every country has their own names for them…This classifying and naming was also a means for humans to gain power. It helped establish boundaries and control over that which had always been predetermined and indeterminable" (Andrews 1993b, pp. 13-4). The tradeoff that comes with classifying and naming spirits is that we may miss out on some of the more subtle experiences that we could otherwise have, because while there is a form of power gained over a spirit by giving it form and substance to work with, there is also a loss of connection and power with that spirit because of how the magician is closing themselves off from the more subtle nuances that a spirit can bring to a relationship. That loss of connection and power demonstrates itself with how people become separated from the wonders of the natural world:

> According to the dispensation of spirit, stones have no agency or experience whatsoever; lichens only have a minimal degree of life; plants have a bit more life, with a rudimentary degree of sensitivity; 'lower' animals are more sentient, yet still stuck in their instincts; 'higher' animals more truly aware – while humans alone in this material world, are really intelligent and *awake*. This way of ordering existence, which depends upon an absolute distinction between matter and spirit, has done much to certify our human dominion over the rest of nature. Although it originates in the ancient Mediterranean and reaches its height in medieval Christianity, this old notion was never really displaced by the scientific revolution. Instead it was translated into a new, up-to-date form by a science still tacitly reliant on the assumption of a limitless human mind (or spirit) investigating a basically determinate natural world (or matter) (Abram 2010 P. 47)

When we can't see the spirits in the world around us, it is not because they aren't part of the world or because they are in a different plane of existence. It is because we have allowed ourselves to get caught up in a narrative about how such beings ought to show up in the world. As a result we miss the more subtle indicators that actually reveal they are already present with us. A stone only seems like in inanimate object, if we filter out the possibility that it could have a life and awareness of its own that is distinctly different our own life and awareness and yet offers something we might learn from. A plant is much more than something growing from the ground. It is a life and a spirit we can connect with, albeit again with a different form of consciousness and awareness than what we are typically used to.

Some of what I'm writing here will be self-evident to many of you, but for some people it may not be and this is no fault on them, but rather an opportunity to recognize the fundamental disconnect we have with the world around us and with spirits, because of how we privilege our human experience over the experience of anything else. For example, we can work with an elemental spirit in an externalized form as a gnome, undine, salamander, or sylph, and this provides us the convenience of a form we can overtly interact with and make sense of. It fits our human needs, allowing us to put the elements into a context that we can relate to. Yet in our need to colonize the elemental spirits with an expectation of a form we can relate too, we are fundamentally denying an essential aspect of what they are and putting them into specific roles that suit us, but also provide a limited connection. The tradeoff is that we don't fully open up to how the elemental spirits might manifest to us, if we didn't limit them with the expectations we bring into the spiritual work we're doing with them:

> These events again caused to question what kind of form was most suitable for visualizing the elementals. In my opinion it is not right to force the world of dwarfs, nixies (water elementals) and fairies into visible forms related to our physical reality. Many people believe it would only need a refinement of our sense of vision to be able to see the ethereal forces of the elemental world, as if normal sight could be upgraded to clairvoyance...this idea of clairvoyance is based on unfounded preconceptions. It rests on the assumption that the human viewpoint is the reference point for all creation, without giving any consideration to the unique differences in the elemental world. Human beings have developed a very definite, refined outer physique, but we display to only a tiny extent how our inner thoughts and feelings operate. In contrast, the elementals are free of

any pre-determined form. They can change their appearance to show what is happening inside themselves, which is very different from our human ways. Whatever form we perceive them in, it is either a mirror which reflects our stored archetypal memory of how we imagine them to be, or it derives from the language of pictures used by the elementals themselves to draw our attention to a certain message they want to deliver. They are without any definite form unless we project archetypal or imagined forms on them. One of these imposed makeshift images is the little gnome with his red pointed cap, his long white beard and leather trousers. Lovers of nature superimpose this picture onto the being of earth spirits (Pogacnik 2009 pp 80-82).

As Pogacnik rightly notes when we limit the elements to the archetypal forms we associate with them, we are only experiencing a minute expression of the elemental spirit. What are we missing out on by only working with the elemental spirit (or any other spirit) in an anthropomorphic form is a more direct experience of their power and essence. We limit it by our need to categorize and define it and while this may provide us power of a sort, it also causes us to miss out on the more subtle and powerful expressions of the elements. Additionally, in anthropomorphizing the spirits we create an artificial hierarchy that benefits us and we see this clearly in the attitude and perspective that is typically shared in regards to elemental spirits, where they are treated as servants. All of this is very convenient for us on one level, but on another level it actually very inconvenient:

It is likely that the 'inner world' of our Western psychological experience, like the supernatural heaven of Christian belief, originates in the loss of our ancestral reciprocity with the animate earth. When the animate powers that surround us are suddenly construed as having less significance than ourselves, when the generative earth is abruptly defined as a determinate object devoid of its own sensations and feelings, then the sense of the wild and multiplicitous otherness (in relation to which human existence has always oriented itself) must migrate, either into a supersensory heaven beyond the natural world, or else into the human skull itself – the only allowable refuge in this world, for what is ineffable and unfathomable (Abram 1996, P. 10).

What anthropomorphism provides us is a way to conceptualize and contain the spirits we work with, in a very convenient way that provides us a sense of power in the defining of those spirits. But anthropomorphism also removes us and them from the raw experience of their power and being and how that is expressed in the world around us, as well as through us. We are not just made up of the mind or emotions, but also the bodily sensations and experiences that we can have, when we fully embrace our place in the world around us. The problem is so many people are removed from the world around them, and it isn't because of where they live, for they elements and spirits are present everywhere. The reason people are so removed is because we've forgotten how to engage with the world around us and be part of it. How do we come back to that?

Perhaps the first thing every human being needs to do in developing an understanding of the Earth's subterranean sphere is to gain a 'sense of place' of where we are at the present moment on the Earth's surface. Does our place in geography affect us physically and spiritually? How does geography express living forces, and how can we become aware of these forces in our daily tasks as striving human beings? We can gain comprehension by developing and understanding and consciousness of the place where we live.

We can study the physical land (geography, geology, mineralogy) to determine the physical character; the bioregion (botany, water, influences of the light and warmth) to determine the etheric character; the cultural heritage (history, indigenous peoples, struggles and wars, and the qualities of pleasure and pain) to determine the astral character; and the question of human destiny (the biography of one's school or business, the influence of the double, and questions coming from the future) to determine the 'I' nature of the place. (Mitchell 2008 pp 15-6).

The suggestions shared above can be a way to come to a better awareness of the place we live in. Certainly making the effort to learn about the land you are part of, the history, the composition and all the other things can bring a person to a more intimate awareness of the land and their place within it. Yet information alone simply isn't enough if we want to connect with the elements on a primal level. We have to be willing to let go of categories and the conceptualizations and step into the real experience with the elements and allow them to connect with us in a way that is very intimate and vulnerable because we are opening ourselves to having a relationship with them where we learn from them and grow with them in a very organic way.

When I started doing research for this book, one of the rhetorical moves that that I found to be fascinating is how some authors would try to associate gravity, electromagnetism and other forces that have been discovered into the 5 classic element model. It was an interesting move because they made the attempt to acknowledge the developments of modern science, while also still trying to keep the classic 5 element model viable. For example, one author made the attempt to associate gravity with the element of earth arguing that "The earth spirits are also a component part of the will of gravity; they are an adhesive between spirit and matter, gravity and levity, and they fashion the solid structures of our planets" (Raven 2012, P. 56). This explanation ultimately comes off as lip service, without really diving into an in-depth exploration of why gravity ought to be associated with the earth element. And while I'll concede a person could associate gravity with earth, I think it's an overreach and ignores the potential for gravity to be an elemental force in its own right. Another example of this conflation occurs with the attempt to associate the elements with time and space:

> The Elements function through time as well. Consider how the Elements express themselves through metabolism, the process of birth, the process of aging, and so on...The Elements are in circulation, within the self, in the greater world, between the within, and without, and more. The Elements traverse the various planes of reality and remain themselves, though they are transformed to adapt to the density and frequency of each plane...Everywhere and everywhen throughout manifest reality, the Elements, as forces and forms, are present as their equivalent of instance objects, as seemingly separate entities based on a common pattern. The Elements are responsible for much of what holds the manifest realm together as a unity. When you work magick of any sort, and particularly elemental magick, it is in part through accessing this web, root-mass, and network that is made of the elemental relationships (Dominguez 2021, pp. 16-7).

While the author makes an excellent point here about the mutable nature of the elemental spirits and how they adapt themselves to the different temporal and spatial aspects of given planes of existence, what I find interesting is that there's no consideration that time and space might be elements themselves. The very fact that time and space are present in the elements speaks to a fundamental aspect of elemental magic, where the elements exist within each other. Why can't time and space be distinct elements?

In the classic 5 model they can't be elements, but if we expand beyond that model and revise our understanding of what elements and elemental spirits are, we can entertain and explore the possibility that space and time could be distinct elemental forces that also play roles in the fundamental building blocks of life. I make this point especially because the author makes another interesting point that I feel further illustrates my argument: "The Elements are part of the substrate and the building blocks for the universe. As such, they exist throughout all of time and space in all planes of reality of the manifest universe. In a real sense, each of the Elements exists in continuous communion with every instance and iteration of itself throughout the vastness" (Dominguez 2021 P. 43). What he has shared applies equally to space and time, if we are open to considering them as elements. It also applies to other types of potential elements that don't quite conveniently fit into the taxonomy of the classic 5 elements, yet nonetheless are too often forced into that taxonomy because it is considered a sacred cow of western occultism.

Another approach that I've seen utilized when it comes to understanding and categorizing the elemental spirits, which I readily appreciate is an attempt to name the elementals by the functional roles they perform (Pogacnik 2009). One example that he shares is that of the elemental of a city. The city is treated as an elemental spirit that interacts with and coordinates the experience of the other elemental spirits, while also insuring the health of the city. It's a novel approach to elemental magic and it fits in with the concept of the egregore or the genii loci, which can be the spirits of cities and countries and corporations (Mace 1998, Stavish 2018). Yet there are specific differences between egregores and elementals. Egregores are much more independent and out for themselves and don't always have the best interests of people or anything else in their focus, because they are perpetuating themselves and the role they perform. A genii loci in comparison fits more readily in with the elemental model and may very well be an advanced elemental being that is tapped into the overall welfare of what it represents, yet it also may not have the best interests of people in mind.

Of course, it could aptly be pointed out that in general we are making an assumption that elementals (or any other types of spirits) give a flying fig about us. They interact with us because we are here, but if they are function based as is suggested by Pogacnik and other authors, we might consider that the main reason they work with us is because we happen to be going along with the functional role they perform, and that if we go against that role they'll either ignore us or respond aggressively. I can vouch for the fact that elementals (and any other type of spirit) are not always kind, cuddly beings that want only the best for us. I once heard a story from a childhood friend where he tried to call up a water elemental, but evidently did so in a manner where it became hostile. He never worked magic again after that because the experience was bad enough to scare him off it, but to me it illustrated that he didn't have a proper grasp of what he was doing or why it is so important to approach spirits from a place of mutual respect and collaboration.

This also brings us back to the question, "What IS an elemental?" In another book, Stephanie Connolly discusses working with daemonic spirits and notes that they are elemental beings (2018). Typically, in most western occultism the overall taxonomy of spirits is separated into distinct categories, of which elementals are one, but why should we assume that this taxonomy is correct? The simple fact is a taxonomy of spirits is at best an interpretation of experiences and observations which SEEMS to indicate what a given spirit is and the function it has, but we ought to question carefully any such taxonomy, including our own, for the simple reason that we don't fully know what a given spirit is or if it has our best interests at heart. We can make observations of the patterns of behavior and the function and the ability of the spirit and think that all of this allows us to know a given spirit, but we ought to consider carefully that what we know is only true up until the moment its proven NOT to be true. The agendas and agencies that we assume about spirits are assumptions and so while it can be quite romantic to paint a picture of the notion that elementals (and other types of spirits) want to evolve by interacting with us, we should critically question that assumption and ask what benefit any spirit really gets from associating with us. We may still ultimately come up with the same answer, but let us get that answer from our own experiences and the careful recording of what we have done or not in pursuit of those experiences.

Part of how we question this assumption is to examine the actual relationship between elementals and humans. To truly work with an elemental involves examining what both parties bring to the relationship. In my observation of western occult communities, what I sometimes see is that many magicians have a tendency to place themselves above the spirits they work with, treating them as servants that are supposed to fulfill their every whim. It doesn't help that the pop culture going back to Goethe's Faust encourages this perspective, as well as of course the various grimoires which are put out and also, for the most part, share a similar perspective. A better approach to working with the elementals (and other spirits) is as a follows:

> For the magician's intelligence is not encompassed *within* the society; its place is at the edge of the community, mediating *between* the human community and the larger community of beings upon which the village depends for its nourishment and sustenance. This larger community includes, along with the humans, the multiple nonhuman entities that constitute the local landscape, from the diverse plants and the myriad animals - birds, mammals, fish,

reptiles, insects - that inhabit or migrate through the region, to the particular winds and weather patterns that inform the local geography, as well as the various landforms - forests, rivers, caves, mountains - that lend their specific character to the surrounding earth. The traditional or tribal shaman, I came to discern, acts as an intermediary between the human community and the larger ecological field, ensuring that there is an appropriate flow of nourishment, not just from the landscape to the human inhabitants, but from the human community back to the local earth [italics are his] (Abram 1996, Pp 6-7).

Most western occultists, upon reading this quoted passage, might protest and say, "But Taylor that's not how the world works now and its not how I engage with the world around me." It's a fair point to make, because for the most part western society doesn't engage or embrace the natural world in the way described, let alone the majority of occultists. Even I can't say that I have embraced the world around me in the way the author described, though I do my best to make such efforts. Nonetheless I think the relationship described above is worth aspiring to and one of the ways we can engage the world around us is to simply go out for a walk and really open ourselves to the experience of the land around us. If you truly want to connect with elemental spirits, this is the best way to connect with them, because they are already present in everything around us. Going out for a walk in your neighborhood or a park or somewhere else can be transformative for you when you open yourself up to experiencing the elemental nature of the world and tap into the respective energies of the elements. And this occurs regardless of what kind of environment you are in. While an urban environment is NOT the same as an environment in the country, you can still feel the wind on your face, connect with the water of rain and puddles and feel the subtle warmth of fire and the steadiness of earth, as well as experiencing the other elemental forces that are present and moving through all of us.

Mediating the relationship between the land and humans should be an essential part of our spiritual journey and work. This mediation can take many forms for the magician, such as performing the role of healer for both the land and people (Abram 1996, Abram 2010, Pogacnik 2007). For instance, when a person is sick that sickness is indicative of an imbalance in their immune system, but it can also be indicative of an imbalance in the environment around them. I don't think its coincidence that the rise in cancer rates has happened as humanity has steadily polluted the environment. What we forget is that we are not above the environment, or the spirits, but rather simply another part of the ecology and environment we live in. We have our own roles to perform, our own functions to execute, but when we put those aside for our own self-interest this helps to create the very imbalance we see within both the environment around us and the one within us. We ideally come back to those roles when we realize that part of our own work involves finding the right equilibrium with the world around us, so that we become part of the environment we live in, instead of placing ourselves in an artificial relationship which can't be sustained in the long run, because after all we are dependent on this world and the forces that sustain it, moreso than they'll ever be reliant upon us. A healthier relationship for humanity, with the spirits, and the world is ironically rooted in how elementals are described as being a smaller representation of the larger whole:

> Spirit or consciousness has to be rooted in energy which has to be rooted in form. If there is a single consciousness that governs the movements of the universe and everything within it, then it also has to be a part of every single form that exists as part of that universe. This train of thought led the Daoists to the conclusion that consciousness resided

within every single thing that exists between the realms of Heaven and Earth, and this consciousness is once again a small part of the greater consciousness which governs all. Like individual cells that make up a larger organism, it is the consciousness within each of us that makes up the larger spirit of existence (Mitchell 2016, PP. 314-15).

When we can acknowledge that we are a smaller part of the whole, it changes our relationship with the spirits. We learn to cultivate an approach where we grow with the spirits, by shifting ourselves out of the human perspective and in the perspective that the spirit provides us (Abram 1996, Pogacnik 2007, Abram 2010). We do this by accepting connection with the spirits in a way that goes outside of our comfort zones, but enables us to experience the world through them. We, in essence, take on the spirit and allow them to teach us through that interaction. This can happen when we learn how to step outside of our everyday consciousness and choose to take on a consciousness that enables us to connect with the nonhuman world, both metaphysically and physically.

Exercise

Go for a walk in your neighborhood or a park and open yourself up to experiencing the elemental spirits. Don't try to anthropomorphize them. Simply open yourself to the experience of them and allow yourself to soak the raw experience in through your bodily awareness. What do you notice as a result?

Share your answers in the magical experiments facebook group #WWES.

How to connect with the elemental spirits directly

When we connect with the elemental spirits, that connection best occurs when we don't treat it as a mental, abstract exercise, but as a real embodied experience that allows us step into the world around us. The problem with many approaches to working with spirits is that we treat them as disembodied beings, and consequently this can cause us to treat ourselves as disembodied beings as well, focused so much on trying to connect with spirits mentally that we forget the inherent power of our bodies, or treat the human body as a mechanistic robotic tool that we have to endure, even though if anything it is exactly a quintessential expression of the elements, and the way spirit has been given flesh to interact with the world that enables us to connect in an intimate and powerful way. We abstract that connection with language, visualization, and other forms of conceptual practices, and what that abstraction ultimately does is removes us from the very connection we're seeking. Yet when we bring our bodies into the mix, to connect with the world, the elementals, and various other spirits, what we discover is that we're part of a collaborative biome, where we both act on and are acted upon by the world and the spirits around us: "As soon as we acknowledge that our hands are included within the tactile world, we are forced to notice this reciprocity: whenever we touch any entity, we are also ourselves being touched by that entity...Such reciprocity is the very structure of perception. We experience the sensuous world only by rendering ourselves vulnerable to that world. Sensory perception is this ongoing interweavement: the terrain enters into us only to the extent that we allow ourselves to be taken up *within* that terrain" (Abram 2010 P. 58). This reciprocity of experience is glossed over in in Western occult spirit practices for the most part and little wonder when we consider the hierarchical approach taken to working with the spirits. Yet when we open ourselves to re-orienting our approach to spirit work so that it becomes a shared experience what is discovered is that the spirits you work with are touching you as much as you are touching them. You are taking on their identities, even as they take on yours. I discovered this when I was 18 and did the exchange of essence with the elementals, but I discover it again each time I work with the spirits. When I go for a walk I connect with the elementals and feel them enter my body even as I enter their awareness. It changes my experience of the world because I can feel the elementals and become part of them even as they take on my experience and become part of me.

One of the ways we can open ourselves to the elemental spirits is to consider how those elemental spirits show up. We treat them like ourselves, as individualized entities, which a humanocentric approach that is convenient for us initially, but ultimately limiting, because we are denying what they are, and the consequent experience we could have, in favor of a limited and shallow relationship (Pogacnik 2007). Instead of just focusing on anthropomorphizing the spirits and expecting them to show up in the form of gnomes, undines, slyphs, salamanders, or some other objectified form, we can go out into the world and experience them directly. Walk out into the sun and then into the shadow and pay attention to each experience. What does each experience provide you spiritually in terms of connecting with the elements? Next look around you, at the trees, grass, hills, or whatever features are available to you. Open yourself to the depths around you, to experience the distance and closeness of things and situate yourself in the land you are part of, and in the elements that make up the land and make up this experience. Instead of objectifying the world, the elements, and everything else we experience, why don't we observe the world, the plants and animals and all the subtle nuances of spiritual contact and saturate ourselves in it, making it part of our being, becoming what is around us and letting that becoming teach us how to relate to the world differently: "To be human is to have a very limited access to what is...The more studiously and apprentice magician watches the other creature from a stance of humility, learning to mimic its cries and to dance its various movements, the more thoroughly his nervous system is joined to another set of senses - thereby gaining a kind of stereoscopic access to the world, a keener perception of the biosphere's manifold depth and dimensionality" (Abram 2010 P. 217). How is this accomplished? By tapping into the world around us and paying attention to its rhythms, but also contributing to this world in a way that isn't intrusive or dominating, but instead is open and curious. When we find a spider in our homes, instead of killing it, how might it feel to gently reach out and carefully bring it outside, so it can continue living, and so can we. One of the ways to honor the elemental and nature spirits involves renegotiating our relationship with the messengers of those beings, our fellow animals, and the plants and other forms of life we cohabitate with. What if you were to make an appropriate offering of food, such bread crumbs or rice grains to the land around you, in order to simultaneously protect your home and come to a better relationships with the life around you? That life has as much right to exist as we do and if we connect with it intimately, we can open ourselves to experiencing the elemental and nature spirits and enter into better relationship with them. They are already around us, with no real need to be summoned overtly. We just have to step out of our own limited perspectives and embrace a different awareness.

One of the ways we do this is by changing our relationship with our bodies. I've discussed some of this work in the Inner Alchemy series, but I think it is just as relevant to our work with the spirits, because when you change the relationship you have with your body, you also change how you experience the world. As long as your body is objectified and treated as a mechanical object that has to be endured, you will never truly connect with any spirit, because the fundamental means of such a connection, your body, is being treated as something to be endured instead of as a gateway to the experiences and wonders of the world around you. Your body isn't some closed structure, but a rather a sensate threshold that is continually interacting with the spirits and the world around you. We see this in the very acts of eating food, defecating, getting sick, and getting back to health. None of these experiences (or others I haven't included) happen in a void. They happen in connection to the world around us and this connection isn't wholly physically. It is also spiritual. The elemental spirits play a role in the experience we have and they do this on an intimate and subtle level that is usually ignored, because we are too often caught up in the "human" experience that we have been sold. But when we step out of that experience, when we humbly acknowledge just how limited that experience is that's when we discover the true depth of our experience and see that it goes much further than what we have limited ourselves to.

Expanding beyond the classic 5 elements

One of the ways we have limited ourselves is by subscribing to a taxonomy of the elemental spirits that only focuses on the 5 classic elements. While at one time this taxonomy made sense, in a way, it has become something that holds us back from experiencing the elemental spirits fully. It has allowed us to categorize and fit the experiences of the elemental spirits and how they apply to this world and universe into 5 categories. For most magicians, perhaps, these five categories work. Yet if we never question them or consider how limiting they actually are or how they may be confining our spiritual work with the elements, what we are left with is a system that is workable, but also has gaps that have never been explored. How do we address these potential gaps?

I would propose an alternate approach to the classic Western model of the 5 elements, where we expand the taxonomy of elemental magic and consider that there may be many more elemental energies/ spirits than what is found in the existing system. If we consider that there are more then we open ourselves to discovery. In the end, you may discover that the classic 5 Western elements is exactly what you need, but you will do so on the basis of having stretched yourself beyond those initial 5 elements and carefully questioning and exploring the alternative. And if in the process you also change you relationship with the spirits and the world around you, this alone will be worth the work you will do by taking on different perspectives that push you outside of the classic model we have access to.

So how do we expand beyond the classic 5 elements? The easiest way to expand beyond the classic five is to consider what else might be considered an elemental force and what makes it an elemental force. If we stick with the definition of elements being the building blocks of life, or we use my definition of the elements being something that moves us and that we move as well, this opens some possibilities for us to explore, because with either definition what we have is some latitude around what an elemental is, as well as what an element is.

For example, gravity could be considered an elemental force. It is a building block of life. It is also a force that moves us and is inescapable. We will always deal with gravity to some degree or another within our lives. Even a person in a space ship is dealing with gravity and needs gravity, in order to maintain bone density and the overall health of the body. Gravity is an elemental force and while it could be argued in the five element model that gravity ought to be part of the earth element, it's distinct enough in its purpose that it could be its own element and worked with as such.

Another example is magnetism, which also can be treated as a separate elemental force. It's again, a building block of life, as well as something that moves our lives. We can apply this same reasoning to electricity, to space, to time, sound/vibration, and various other aspects of physical reality that we deal with every day, which when treated as separate and distinct elemental forces and spirits, provides opportunities beyond what is available in the five elemental model.

However, we also don't have to limit ourselves to just physical forces. When we are dealing with elemental spirits and powers, we're dealing with the metaphysical as well. Stillness can be an elemental power or experience just as movement can be. These are two quintessential aspects of our lives that we deal with each day that play a role in how we live our lives, but also in the building of the universe and the balancing of that universe. Likewise love can be treated as an elemental force, because while it can be labeled as an emotion, it also had depths and dimensions that go beyond just an emotional feeling. Wars have been fought in regards to love and that says a lot about love as an elemental force.

At this point you may justifiably be thinking to yourself, "But where does this stop Taylor? How many elemental spirits and types do we come up with?" Part of that is dependent upon you and how flexible you want to get with definition of what an elemental power is. In the next chapter I'm going to walk you through my work with the elemental balancing ritual and describe the various elements I've worked with over the years. You don't have to work with the same elements I've worked with, but I think it can be fruitful to explore working with different elements. With that thought in mind, let me share the final exercise of this chapter.

Exercise

For this exercise you're going to actually create elemental portals for elementals that aren't the classic five elements. You'll create both the elemental portal and the spiritual portal for the element. To create these portals you'll need to connect with the element and start working with it. I've shared a couple examples of portals below that I came up with for gravity and magnetism. My version of gravity has the colors of Green and Black associated with it and my version of magnetism has blue, purple, yellow, green, red, black, and orange. As I've written above, come up with your own versions of the color associations with the elements.

What I did to make initial connection with these elements as work with the element of quintessence, since it contains all other elements. I asked that elemental power to help me connect with gravity, magnetism and other elements and when I made those connections, I then requested the elemental and spiritual portal from the spiritual representative of the element. Once this information was provided I created the portals and used them to strengthen my connection with the element.

After you've created portals for the non-classic elements, work with them doing pathworkings and rituals. What do you notice when you work with these elements? Is there a difference in working with them as opposed to the classic elements or is it a similar experience? Does working with these elements change your experience and understanding of them and if so how?

You can also come up with other correspondences. For example, you can come up with an elemental sound for gravity, magnetism, or other elements. Those sounds don't have to be vowels. For example I use the sound of ZZZZ for working with the element of time. We can take the same technology and methodology with the classic elements and apply it to the modern elements, or not, depending on what you want to do, but regardless don't be afraid to experiment with other elements outside the classic 5, to see what you learn and experience as a result.

Share your answers in the magical experiments facebook group #WWES.

Conclusion

One of the more underused aspects of elemental magic is around how elemental magic can be applied to internal work. The next chapter is a system I developed in 2004 and have continued to work with for the last 18 years of my life and have used to do internal work. I also think it provides an excellent way to truly get to know elemental powers and apply them to your life.

Chapter 4: The Elemental Balancing Ritual

In 2004, I had a dream that caused a pivotal change in direction in the course of my life. I dreamt that if I continued on the course that I was on, I would end up putting myself into a situation where I would end up in jail. I was still going through a self-destructive phase at the time and the dream was a wakeup call that I needed to find some way to shift course. I had already done some therapy over the years, but therapy alone, in my case, wasn't enough. Fortunately a friend of mine turned me on to Taoist breathing meditation practices and those practices helped me start working through some of the deeper traumas and blockages I had embedded in my overall being. However, I also develop a practice of my own that I have continued to use for the last 18 years (at the time of this writing). This practice is the elemental balancing ritual, and although I've written about it in other books, I'm revisiting it here because of how it pertains to the elemental magical work we are doing in this book.

I developed the elemental balancing ritual, because I recognized that it was possible to work with the elemental spirits and elemental energies in a way that brought balance into one's life. The first element I worked with was the element of water. I chose water because I felt out of all the elements it would help me get in touch with my emotions and learn how to feel them in a way that was healthy, instead of acting them out in an unhealthy way. For one year I worked with the element of water, each and every day, seeking to get to know the element, as well as apply it to my life in a way that would help me find the balance I was seeking. By the end of that year I had become more flexible mentally and emotionally and much more in touch with my emotions than I had ever been. I realized that working with the elements in this way could help a person achieve a healthier balance with their overall life, and decided to continue pursuing this as a lifelong practice. Before I share the other elements I have worked with, I am going to describe the original process I developed to connect with and attune to an element as well as what the daily practice looked like.

Ritual: Elemental Balancing Ritual Attunement and Daily Work

For this ritual you need to first pick the element you are going to work with. I recommend working with one of the original 5 elements in any of the systems that have been shared earlier in the book, because you'll already be familiar with those elements. You may find it useful to meditate on a specific element for a few days to see if it's the element you want to work with. I would recommend working with the elemental portals, meditating first on the elemental portal and then the spiritual portal for the element, so that you can to the elemental plane.

First pick up the elemental portal and stare at it for a few minutes, letting it saturate your awareness. When you are ready, project your consciousness in to the elemental portal. Then visualize a tunnel. The tunnel leads you to the spiritual portal for the elemental energies. Pick that portal up and spend a few minutes staring at it, saturating your consciousness with it. When you are ready project yourself into the spiritual portal, visualize the door opening and step into the elemental plane of existence.

Once you are in the elemental plane of existence, an elemental spirit will present itself. Ask that it present itself in a form you can connect with. Depending on the element you work, it may appear in the form of a gnome, sylph, salamander, or naga, or it may appear in a form that is relevant to you. For example, when I worked with the element of water, the elemental spirit appeared as Spike Spiegel from Cowboy Bebop. Whatever form the elemental spirit appears is in is the form it will take as it works with you through the year. Ask the elemental spirit for a personal symbol that you can use to invoke the elemental energy into you on the night you'll do the elemental balancing ritual. Once the symbol is provided thank the spirit and return through the portals.

For the night when you'll do the attunement ritual, you will need the following:

Body paint with the specific color of the element

Oil that represents the elemental energy

Candles for the color of the element

A personalized invocation of the element you'll be working with, as well as personalized chants for the quarters[1].

An offering for each of the elements that is personalized for each of them.

On the night of the ritual, you will first call the quarters using the personalized chants you've developed. You'll also make the offering for each element in the relevant directions. Then you will go to the center of the circle you have cast. Light the candles that represent the element you have chosen to work with. You will anoint your head with the oil that represents the elemental energy and paint the elemental symbol you received on your forehead. You will invoke the elemental spirit that you have worked with. Once the elemental spirit is invoked, you will ask it to become your guide for the next year and help you achieve balance with the element it represents. Commune with the spirit until you feel that you've established a strong connection. Ask it for instructions on how to work with it each day and bring it into your life. Once you have the instructions, close the circle by thanking the spirits and putting out the candles.

For the daily practice, you will invoke the elemental spirit you are working with. You can do this in a meditative trance, using the symbol given to you to help you invoke the spirit. Once the spirit is invoked, go about the rest of your day, but keep yourself open and receptive to any advice or intuitive pings that the spirits gives you around the element you are working or any advice on how to balance your life. You may also end up getting some insights on how to work with the element magically and mundanely.

For instance when I worked with Water, I got a lot of advice about emotional flexibility and receptivity, but also advice on staying hydrated and drinking more water. I also learned to work with the fluids in my body, as well as working with fluids around me. That year long work taught me a lot about water and my relationship with it and to this day I have a deeper understanding and relationship with water that I would not have otherwise.

When it's time to transition from one element to another, you'll do a closing ritual for the first element. The next evening you'll do the same ritual I shared above, but to the next element you want to work with.

The closing ritual is fairly simply. You'll get four colored candles that represent the element you are closing the ritual to. You'll call your circle, then you'll light the candles and call in the elemental spirit you worked with. You want to thank that spirit and the element. I recommend coming up with a farewell chant and an offering. You will ask the elemental spirit to continue working in the background to bring balance and insight to your life. It's important to recognize that you have formed a lifelong connection to the element, because of the work you've done. You're no longer making that element the primary focus of your spiritual and internal work, but you have made it a part of your life in a way that goes beyond just doing a ritual to the element in an evening. You worked with it for an entire year (or more) and that work changed your life.

Two pieces of advice I want to offer in regards to this work. First keep a journal where you chart the changes in your life as a result of working with the element. Keeping a journal will allow you to see the changes objectively, and help you understand how the elemental work has transformed your life.

The second piece of advice is this: Don't enter into this work lightly. This type of work is intense, demanding and it WILL change your life and the lives of people around you. You are choosing to work with an elemental energy and spirit in order to bring balance to your life. The overall effects will ultimately be beneficial, but a lot of changes come with this work. My first ex-wife once complained to me about this work, asking why I had to do it, especially because of how it changed things between us. My response was that such changes were probably inevitable, but also that by doing this work I was proactively seeking to change myself and become a better person. When you do this kind of work, you will change who you are and you may grow away from the people you are with. If despite that possibility the work is worth doing, then do it because it will transform your life, but go into this work with your eyes open, recognizing that some change will inevitably occur.

Analysis of the original ritual

I've shared the original ritual, in this book, for a few reasons. The first reason is that it, and the daily practice, are easy to replicate and a great way to start the elemental balancing ritual. I do recommend picking one of the 5 elements, of whatever system you want to work with, because you're likely already familiar with those elements, and it will help you dip your toes into using elemental magic for internal work.

The second reason I included the original ritual, it that it has changed me for quite a bit since I first did it. I will describe those changes below in more depth, but I wanted you to see what the original working was like, as a comparison and to also illustrate how a given magical working can change over the years as your practice changes, and the way you work with a given spiritual force changes.

The final reason I wanted to share this ritual is that it a good example of an anthropomorphic ritual. Meeting the elemental spirit and asking it to take a form that is familiar to you is essentially an anthropomorphic ritual. There's nothing wrong with that, but I make that point because as you'll see in the later version of this work, that aspect is stripped out altogether. Before we get to that I want to share what else changed and how doing this work lead me to working with non-traditional elemental spirits.

The Evolution of the Elemental Balancing Ritual

After I finished working with water for the year, I decided that I next needed to work on my communication skills and becoming more assertive. At first I contemplated working with the element of air. After all it is the element that is typically associated with communication. It would have made sense to have worked with it, but it didn't quite feel right. Neither did earth, fire nor spirit. I was stumped because I knew where I needed some balance and some help, but none of the elements quite fit what I was looking for. I could have tried to force a fit, but that didn't feel right either. I spent some time meditating on the matter and came to the conclusion that I needed to work with sound (vibration) as an element. The problem was that sound wasn't typically treated as an element.

I decided that I needed to be open to the possibility that sound could be an element, and treat it as such. It's a building block of the universe and it moves us, even as we move it. I did the same elemental balancing ritual attunement and invocation that I shared above and I discovered that I was able to connect with sound as an element. For the next year I worked with sound and became a better communicator and more assertive, while also learning about the elemental powers of sound. The biggest lesson I learned though was that I didn't need to restrict myself to the classic 5 elements. There were more elements out there that could be worked with and I decided I would work with them. I shared this realization with several other people who had chosen to do the elemental balancing ritual and they also began to experimenting with working outside of the classic 5 elements. All of us found that we were able to do meaningful and profound work with the elements that we worked with that didn't fit into the classic 5 elements, and still continue working with the traditional 5 as well.

Here's a list of the elements I have done the elemental balancing ritual work with: Water, Sound/Vibration, Earth, Love, Emptiness, Identity, Movement, Stillness, Fire, Creativity, Space, Time and Connection/Truth. I want to note that I have worked with other elements outside of the elemental balancing ritual, but these are the elements I've worked, for internal work. In some cases, I have worked with a given element for multiple years, and this was another change that came to elemental balancing ritual.

Initially the ritual was designed to focus on an element for a year. However, in some cases, I realized I needed to work with an element for longer than a year. I decided to change the protocol of the work and start working with a given element for longer. In the case of creativity, and movement I worked with those elements for two years, while in the case of stillness, I worked with it for 3 years. In each case where further work was warranted it made sense to me that I would work with the element further, because there was more internal work to do with the element.

In some cases, such as with love, identity and creativity, it could be argued that these aren't really building blocks of life. However they are forces that move us. Admittedly they aren't physical forces, but I don't think we should limit the elements to purely physical forces either. Working with these elements demonstrated to me that they were just as essential to work with as the more physical elements, because of the necessary balance that can be achieved in working with them and what could be learned about them as elements.

Another change that occurred in the evolution of this work is how elements are picked. Initially, in the first few years, I would pick the element myself. However as I continued to do the elemental balancing ritual, I found that the next element would reveal itself to me partway through the year, in a way that was more intuitive and spoke directly to what I really needed to work on within my life. For instance I moved from stillness to creativity, when it became clear that I had hit a place of creative block. This came to me through a flash of insight, and was quite different from me arbitrarily picking the element. That insight made it clear I needed to find a different balance with my creativity.

A final change which occurred is that I eventually stopped anthropomorphizing the elements and the elemental spirits. Instead of doing the ritual I shared above, I came up with a ritual where I invoked the element directly into myself and switched from one elemental force to another. This change in the ritual didn't happen for a number of years, but when it did I stopped with a spirit as a representative of the element and started working with the element directly. I would suggest for anyone new to this work and wanting to embody an element that they first do the initial anthropomorphic work for at least a couple of years, in order to get used to the experience of working with an element. Directly working with an element in the manner I'm about to describe requires a certain amount of spiritual stamina that simply can't be achieved without having first laid down some groundwork, especially because of how intense this work can get.

Ritual: The Embodied Elemental Invocation

In the embodied elemental invocation, we no longer work with an anthropomorphized version of the elemental spirit. Instead what we seek to do is work with the element as directly as possible, bringing in the elemental current or energy in order to transform our lives and find balance with that current. This is a direct mediation of the elemental energies, as opposed to working with a representative that mediates the energies for you.

The advantage of working with a representative (aside from making the working more humanocentric) is that the representative does mediate the element energy and makes sure you don't take on too much. This is why I do recommend initially doing the original ritual, and you may find that you only ever do that ritual with this work and if so that's fine. However as you become more acclimated to elemental energies you may find that you can work with them more directly and that you may prefer to take on an embodied experience where you bring the elemental energy in and work with it as directly as possible.

For this ritual, you can create and use elemental portals as I've described in chapter three, as well as using appropriate candles and even coming up with a personalized sigil to represent the element. All of these tools can serve the purpose of helping you attune to the element. Or you can simply do the working without all of these tools, if you are already sensitized to the elemental energies. I'll present both versions below and walk you through how they work.

Embodied Elemental Ritual with Tools

For this ritual you will lay out the elemental portal and the spiritual portal for the element you are going to work with. Between those portals, you will place the candles, but don't light them. Paint the personalized symbol on your forehead. Then do your standard circle raising ritual. Once your circle is raised, light each of the candles. Sit down and look at the elemental portal first, meditating on it to attune yourself to how the elemental energies show up in the world. You may, if you want, recite an invocation of the element as well that you've personally created for it.

Once you feel attuned to the elemental portal, switch your focus to the spiritual portal for the element. Meditate on it to attune yourself to the spiritual energies of the element and connect with the elemental plane of existence. You may, if you want, recite an invocation of the spiritual aspects of the element that you've personally created for it.

When you are attuned to the spiritual portal, focus on both the elemental and spiritual portals. You want to draw the spiritual energy of the element to you and your body, from the spiritual portal, through the elemental portal, so that it flows into your body and consciousness becoming part of your energetic and spiritual matrix. Don't fight the energy. If you are fighting it, it means you aren't ready to do this work, and should go back to doing the original ritual I shared above. The elemental energies should mesh with you and become part of you, something you are mediating directly in order to bring balance in your life with that element, but also as a way of establishing deeper relationship with the element. You will experience the element much more directly than if you're working with a spirit because it will become part of your energy that you are mediating into the environment around you, as well as within your internal reality.

The daily work with the element will be similar to the daily work done in the previous version of the ritual, but instead of having an elemental spirit offer advice and perspective, you'll get direct intuitive insights from the elemental essence itself. You may find yourself thinking of how you would approach a situation from the elemental perspective or you may apply the elemental energy to a situation in order to change and balance it with the element. For example, my work with Creativity inspired me to come up with ways to shape my environment creatively with my art, while also setting up a life time of writing projects that I will hopefully get to. Mediating that creative energy changed my life and helped me realize my creative potential in ways I had previously ignored.

Embodied Elemental Ritual without Tools

This ritual is the same as the above, but you aren't using any tools. Instead you are simply meditating and attuning yourself to the elemental and spiritual energies you have chosen to work. You will be able to feel a direct connection to the element because of the prior work you've done with other elements and because the element you are working with has made itself known in your life and its clear to you that need to work with it. When you meditate on the element you are going to focus on the experiential aspect of working with it and how your body and spirit respond to the elemental energies. This will guide you to connect with the element directly.

With both this version and the one with tools, you may find it useful to also create an artistic expression of the element, while doing the ritual. If you do this, have a paintbrush or two on hand, as well as whatever medium of paint and palette you prefer. You'll create the painting as an evocation of the elemental and spiritual energies of the element that can be used to further connect with the element as well as embody it in your physical space. It serves a similar purpose to the elemental portals you create, but it also an expression and evocation of yourself and your fusion with the elemental energy.

Analysis of the Ritual

As you can see this ritual is quite different from the original ritual. Even the tools version is different because of how it incorporates the elemental and spiritual portals into the work. The focus of this work is to create an embodied experience of the element and you will need to have a foundation in place for this kind of work because that foundation will have enabled you to become more sensitized to the elemental energies in general. You will be able to distinguish and recognize the different elemental energies and embody them through your physical, energetic, and spiritual bodies, bringing yourself into balance with the element as well as mediating into the world around you.

I want to note that you don't have to revisit your prior work with previous elements and do this version of the ritual with them. You can if you want to, but you have essentially mediated that energy in your life and made it part of who you are. This version of the work is simply a more direct experience. It's not essential to do, and it's up to you how far you want to take this work. I've included it here, because it's how I currently do the elemental balancing ritual, and because I think it's good to show the evolution of a magical working and how it can change, especially if you continue to work it in your life consistently.

Conclusion

The elemental balancing ritual changed my life. It helped me steer my life into a better direction than it was going and transformed my relationship with the elements even further. It introduced me to the simple fact that there are many more elements out there than just the classic five elements. There's definitely been some changes that have occurred along the way that initially didn't seem optimal. I have questioned doing this work sometimes because the balance that was achieved came at the cost of relationships in my life. Yet nonetheless when I look back at the overall work what strikes me is that my life has become steadier and better overall. Doing this work has allowed me to turn the lead of my life into gold. I don't know that it could be done any easier than it has been, and sometimes to do the work, one must necessarily accept that what the work brings with it is a simple truth: What you put into the work is what you get out of it, but what you get out of the work may change you in ways you could never anticipate, but that you actually needed.

Chapter 5: How to Walk with Elemental Spirits

This book is titled "Walking with Elemental Spirits" and the entire series has a similar focus to it. When I use the term walk with spirits I am referring to the notion that a person can walk with the spirits literally, because the spirits are around us all the time. To walk with the spirits is to enter a deliberate relationship with them where we invite them into our lives as collaborators that we work with. When we walk with spirits, we aren't trying to have power over them, so much as power with them, and we are inviting them into our lives, even as we, in turn, are being invited in their existence. So what does walking with elemental spirits look like?

The elemental balancing ritual provides you a taste of what that looks like, for in working with a given element so intimately you end up discovering a lot about how that element works and how you can work with it, but you also transform your understanding of yourself, in relationship to that element. This is how magic ought to work, both with and without working with spirits. If we never change who we are in relationship to the work we are doing and/or change our relationship with the world and universe around us, we are missing out on something fundamental to magic, and living life. We don't exist in a vacuum and the relationships that we have, both material and spiritual, play a significant role in the evolution of who we are.

Nonetheless when I talk about with the elemental spirits, I am talking about literally going for a walk in order to connect with the elemental spirits. This isn't a walk where you are cogitating about the latest issues in your life, for while the elemental spirits are around you simply aren't able to focus on them, when you are focused on whatever is bugging you. A walk with the elemental spirits is a deliberate choice to focus on connecting with both the environment around you and the environment of your body. Each step you take, each movement that you make becomes part of this awareness you develop when connecting with the elements so deliberately.

I have done this practice myself for all of my adult life. I remember going for hikes in the local parking and opening my awareness to the elements around me, feeling their awareness touch on mine and show me the hidden layers of the world. In recent years, this practice has become more deliberate on my part, in that I have started to include qi gong and bua gua practices into my walking in order to deepen this experience of walking with the elemental spirits. Integrating these practices into my walks has allowed me to deepen this kind of experience and open myself to further mediation of the elemental energies in the area.

The one difference between this practice and the elemental balancing ritual is that I am not focused on mediating a specific element, so much as mediating all of the elemental energies that are in the area. However this mediation still requires a level of focused awareness that allows me to distinguish between the different elemental energies that are being taken in and worked with. You can also choose to just focus on working on one specific elemental energy if you want to. I don't, but that's because my interest is in learning to work with multiple elemental energies and mediate them through me.

Before we continue with the practice, I want to briefly speak to what mediation is. Mediation, in this context, is a process where you take in and work with specific energies in order to integrate them into yourself, and also channel them into the world around you. In the case of elemental energies, one could say, "But Taylor, aren't these energies already in the environment? Why do we need to mediate them?" These are fair questions to ask. In truth it could be argued that the different expressions of spirits are already present in the environment, so this question can be applied to those expressions as well. Yet there are good reasons to mediate the spirits and energies they represent, precisely because we have something they don't: A physical embodied presence. The physical manifestation of ourselves allows us to mediate these energies and bring them into further alignment with the world around us. It also allows us to do the work of refining our own internal energy, freeing us from the blockages and tensions of not only our own lives, but also the ancestral patterns, and possible past live patterns we've brought in. I can't speak to what the ultimate goal of all this work is, because it will differ from person to person. Some people will do this work in the hopes of "evolving" past a material existence, while other people, myself included, will do it because we recognize that we may come back again, but in the process of death and transformation, we want to take all of these experiences and bring them back to the totality of the universe, before we come back around for another round of life. Whatever the reason is that you are doing this work, mediation is a powerful means of taking in energies and acclimating them to your body and spirit, while also expressing into the world through the filter that you are.

So is this process as simple as going out for a walk and soaking in nature? Not quite. Even when I was younger that wasn't exactly what I was doing. When I go for a walk, I would extend my sensorial awareness, both psychic and physical to the world around me, with a focus on connecting with what was around me. I was going for a walk, but I was also actively connecting to the world around me, and as such was not caught up in my own thoughts or feelings, which would be a distraction. Sometimes, when people go for walks, they aren't taking anything in around them. They are in their heads, and perhaps hearts, working through whatever is going on in their lives, or at least thinking about it. Walking with spirits, elemental, or otherwise calls for you to have a sufficiently peaceful awareness with yourself, so you can focus that awareness on other things. If you are caught up in your own thoughts and emotions you won't have the capacity to connect with anything else in a meaningful way or recognize that something is trying to connect with you. Earlier in the book, I asked that you go for a walk and record your experiences. We're going to use that initial experience as a comparison to the exercise you are going to do now.

Exercise

I want you to go for a walk, in a park, or your neighborhood or multiple places if you want to do this exercise more than once (I heartily recommend that by the way). When you walk, I want you to focus on extending your sensorial awareness, both psychic and physical, to the environment around you. Open yourself to connecting to whatever is present, with the caveat that if the connection doesn't feel right, feel free to shut that connection down. What impressions and experiences do you pick up? What does your awareness of this experience tell you about the elemental and spiritual energies you are connecting with? Compare this experience to your initial experience. What if, anything is different?

Share your answers in the magical experiments facebook group #WWES.

Integrating Qi Gong into your Walks

Going for a walk where you extend your awareness outward and really connect with the elemental spirits can seem like a fairly simple exercise to do, but how many people really do this? From what I can tell, not many people actually do something like this, so I hope that you take this seriously and really attempt it, because it will change your relationship with the elementals that you connect with. They are not used to us connecting with them in this way, so when it happens what I've discovered is that they are much more responsive.

In the last couple of years, I've added Qi Gong to this process, specifically drawing on the practices of Bua Gua for doing walking meditation and mediation, but also using the standing meditations and other practices I've learned to help me become more attuned to the environment around me, and specifically to the elemental energies that are present in that environment. Such practices, while they take you within yourself, also make you more aware of the environment around you and it's that awareness we want to cultivate in order to more fully connect with the elements.

So how do you apply Qi Gong and Bua Gua to this work? First, let's start with a standing practice. Stand with your feet parallel to each other. Slightly "sit" your hips so that your thighs go backward, just a bit, and you are lightly resting your body on your feet. Your arms should be at your side, palms facing towards you back. Slightly tuck your chin, so your neck straightens, with the rest of your back. For the next twenty minutes just stand this way, aligning your body until it feels comfortable and you are simply aware of yourself. Then, once you are ready, extend your awareness outward, below your feet, above your head, and to the environment around you. You may or may not notice a subtle feeling of qi coming into you from the environment. Regardless of what you do or don't feel, continue extending your awareness outward, while still maintaining awareness of your body. If you find yourself spacing out or losing awareness of your body or the environment around you, start over again and bring yourself back to awareness.

This is a good way to do standing practice, cultivate awareness of your qi and awareness of the environment of the elemental energies around you. After each standing session take a few moments to record your observations. What did you notice about your body and how it connected with the elemental energies and environment? Where did you feel a sense of blockage or tension that might be getting in the way of the connection? What communication, in whatever form, came through? This may seem like a simple exercise, but what you are learning to do here is embody your awareness in the experiences you are having and thus learning to pick up on the subtle forms of communication that occur every day between yourself and the environment around you. We have blocked these subtle forms of communication out, because of the media environment we live in and the expectation to conform to a mainstream society, but we can open ourselves to them again, by learning how to pay attention to the subtle nuances of communication. This exercise teaches you that. You can do it inside your home or office, but also outside in a park or in your yard.

Once you've done this standing practice for a month, then you are ready to go to the next step. Why a month? First, because you need to spend some time cultivating awareness and if you've never done that up until now, then trying to do anything else simply will not work. Second, it disciplines you and teaches you how to tap into and become more aware of both your body (physical, energetic, and spiritual) and how the environmental and elemental energies communicate with your body.

Now let's proceed to integrate walking into this work. With walking practice, you aren't walking the normal way you usually do. If you are walking the way you normally do, you will likely be distracted with whatever thoughts and emotions are going through your mind or with the need to reach a destination. That's what normally occurs with walking, but we're not walking to reach a destination or work through whatever thoughts and emotions are occurring. We're walking for the purpose of connection with the elemental energies and awareness of that interaction in the body. We are experientially embodying the connection between the elements and ourselves.

The practice of Bua Gua, which is Taoist walking meditation, can be useful for this kind of connection with the elements. I'm going to share some of the basics of this practice, but also recommend that you check out energyarts.com to get more information and take classes that will help you learn Bua Gua, if you decide you want to practice it.

With Bua Gua, when you walk, you are doing what's called mud walking, because you are walking slowly, as if you were walking in mud. What you are attempting to do is draw on the qi of the earth, with each step. When you step, you step with your heel leading and then your toes touching the ground. Each step is done slowly. The preceding foot steps to meet the first foot and then steps ahead. So if you step with your left foot, then you would move your right foot to be parallel to your left foot and then step again with your right foot. Then you'd bring your left foot forward to be parallel to your right foot and then step forward with your right foot. You repeat this with each step and as you can see this is quite different from how people normally walk. It deliberately forces you to slow down and focus on the act of walking, but also gets you to pay attention to the sensation of qi, and if you choose, the other sensations, including connecting with the elemental spirits.

While you are walking, you can also be doing something with your hands and arms. For example, when I'm warming up, I will start with my and arms at my side, with my palms facing down. When I take a couple steps, I'll raise my arms, until they are at the level of my heart and I'll place the palms facing inward (though you can also have them facing outward). I'll take a few more steps and raise my arms further, with the palms facing upward at the level of my head, and then take a few more steps and bring my forearms together, with the palms facing inward at the level of my face. These basic arm postures serve to help raise the qi and active the three Tiens, which are the energetic cauldrons of the body, located at the navel, heart, and head.

There are other movements that can be done with Bua Gua, but they are too complicated to go into here in this book. However if you practice the basic movements I've described and use them to sensitize you to the elemental energies and spirits, you'll find this practice can help you mediate and work with elemental energies as you walk.

During the spring and summer of 2021, I spent a lot of time developing this practice of integrating the elements into my walking meditation. I would go for a walk on a park path and start doing the Bua Gua walking and doing the arm postures I described. I focused initially on just feeling the qi circulate in my body and connecting to the environment around me. Once I really sunk into the practice, then I would invite the elemental spirits to come and work through me. I mediate their energy and essence as I walk, and in that process they communicate with me as well, sharing their insights as well as helping me channel their energies for the purposes of doing practical magical work as well as work for the elements.

This practice will take some time to develop. I am still refining it and improving on it at the time of this writing, but I've shared it here because it is the evolution of my work with elements, and with mediating the energy of spirits in general. It's also part of the experiential embodiment work I've been developing, with the focus in this case being on experientially embodying the elemental energies in the environment.

When you do the Bua Gua walking focus first on simply being aware of the movement of your walking and your environment. Any thoughts and emotions that come up should be gracefully recognized and then let go of. As your awareness of yourself and the environment increases, focus on the sensation of qi, cultivating both the awareness of your own qi and the qi of the environment. When you feel the energetic sensations of the qi, extend your awareness outward to invite in the elemental energies and meet them at the level of reciprocity they are willing to give you. Continue the walking, allowing the spirits in and mediating their energies through your awareness of them. You may feel some adjustments of your own energy as you mediate the elemental energies. Allow yourself to be open to the adjustments, as what is happening is that the elemental spirits are making it easier for you to process their energies. I recommend doing this work consistently. This is a meditative practice and what you'll get out of it will be continual insights into the elemental spirits, as well as how to balance your energy with the elements.

The Invitation

One thing I briefly mentioned above was inviting the elemental spirits and energies in. One of the things I've been working on, both with spirit work, and life in general is making myself more aware of the level of invitation that has been extended for a connection, whether it's with a spirit or a person. In other words, you may want to go in connect as deeply as possible, but that isn't necessarily the right connection for the moment. I've had this realization myself, in the wake of reinventing my own life, because sometimes I've gone for depth, instead of actually connecting with someone or something on the level that they are most comfortable with. In spirit work this concept of invitation is important because it serves to remind us of honoring our own boundaries with regards to the spirit and being able to set the level of connection according to what is best for the individual practitioner and for that matter the spirit. I think it's important to cultivate this kind of awareness because learning to actually feel into the connection and know where to come to a consensus with the spirit you connect can help you develop a more powerful relationship with that spirit, but also with your own sense of sovereignty. Learning to connect to the depth you where you are invited to connect can make a significant difference in the efficacy of the connection and the overall experience that happens.

Going deep is not always the best approach and may not even be that deep because your perception is oriented only toward what you think is deep, when actually you're still in the shallows because the awareness isn't focused on the connection but what you want out of the connection. That's an important distinction to make because when you have that realization you discover how subjective the experience is and how that subjectivity can stop you from really connecting in a meaningful way, based on being aware of the invitation that has been extended.

In western magic there is either this tendency to expect that spirits will come when called and that we can dictate the relationship with the spirits, or on the other end, the spirits get to dictate the relationship. In truth, it's better to take a middle path, where you recognize that both sides of the relationship have some power and say over the depth of connection and what the actual relationship will look like. This awareness encourages a collaborative consensual between yourself and the spirits you work with.

When you take the approach of being aware that you've been extended an invitation, what you recognize in turn is that an invitation is an offer to connect at the right level for the moment of that invitation. This matters in our spiritual work and our lives, because when we connect from a place of mutual consensus there is synchronicity found in that connection which strengthens the spiritual working (or whatever else) and offers the potential for genuine deeper connections down the line. Relationships don't happen in a moment. They take time to build and deepen and this is true whether you are making friends with another person or connecting with a spirit. So keep this in mind as you work with elemental spirits, spirits in general, as well as the people you meet. You might be surprised at how much easier life is when you make the effort to be aware of the appropriate level of communication and connection that each party seeks in whatever the circumstances are.

Conclusion

The walking practice I've shared is an easy one to gloss over, but it is perhaps the most rewarding method of communicating with the spirits, because it teaches you how to connect with them using your awareness. It's a practice I'll keep coming back to in each book of this series and its one I recommend spending some time with because of how it will help you become more attuned to the subtleties of the spirits and how they connect with people, outside of how we expect them to connect with us.

Chapter 6: How to Heal with Elemental Magic

One of the ways that I like to work with elemental magic involves working with the elementals to heal yourself. First I need to make a brief disclaimer. What I share is not intended as medical advice or to replace the advice and care you would get from a doctor. It can be considered supplemental advice, but you should continue to get advice from a medical professional if you have a situation you are dealing with or get that advice and help if a situation develops. With that disclaimer made, let's focus on how to work with elemental spirits and magic for the purposes of healing and health.

In chapter 4, I talked about the elemental balancing ritual. While that ritual is mainly focused around doing internal work with your issues and also seeking balance with the elemental energies in general, what should be remembered is that the internal work does have a physical health component to it. After all, the stressors of our lives do play a role in how well or poorly we sleep, as well as other life choices that we make. The elemental magic work we do can play a role in how we manage those stressors and actually help us lead healthier lives, and we already have access to the elementals, because of the fact that the human body is, in part, comprised of the elements in and of itself.

One of the reasons I mediate the elemental energies is to apply them to my body and use the elemental currents to help with the process of keeping my body healthy. And if you practice qi going, you can also learn specific exercises and movements that are also helpful for stimulating the elemental energies, because of how qi gong teaches you to connect with the elements around you.

Pogacnik also shared an interesting idea in his books, namely that an elemental is assigned to each person, to help with the health of the body (2009, 2016). While I'm not entirely convinced on that particular idea, especially because the elemental assigned would be limited by its nature, I do think it's important to recognize that we already have an innate access to the elemental energies. If we just apply the classic 5 element model to the human we have the element of earth associated with the flesh and bones, the element of water associated with the liquids of the body, the element of fire associated with the muscles of the body, the element of air associated with the oxygen coming into the body and the element of quintessence associated with the spirit/soul of the body. If we apply my model of elemental magic to the mix then this expands further into other aspects of the body such as the nervous system. The Eastern systems have their perspective on this as well, which can be found in Ayurveda and also in Qi Gong. Regardless of what model you apply to yourself, the point is that you can use elemental energies and spirits for healing your body, or healing other people, so let's look at how that might work.

The Cycle of Life

Healing yourself with elemental energies fundamentally involves developing a relationship with your body that tunes you into what is going on with your body, and helps you recognize when there are irregularities with the body that need to be addressed. My *Inner Alchemy* series offers some help in this regards, but I also want to share how the elemental magic work you do can help you with this work. If you've started doing the standing and walking practices I've shared in previous chapters, you may already be noticing where you don't necessarily feel as healthy as you could be feeling. Some of this awareness will be physical, based on the aches and pains that you feel, or a general sense of unhealthiness. Some of this awareness will be energetic and spiritual. Perhaps you feel a sense of blockage and tension? All of these details should be paid attention to, because they can provide crucial information that can help you make life style changes that can greatly enhance your health.

Now life style changes may not seem very glamorous or magical, but I think health is rooted in how we take care of ourselves. The choices we make in terms of the food we eat, what we drink, how much we exercise and all the other relevant details play a significant in the health of our lives, and if we take a proactive approach we can live healthier and longer lives, because of how we're choosing to take care of ourselves. The elemental spirits respond to that because of their respective roles and functions which focus on the sustainment of life. However what we should also remember is that the elements don't just create but also destroy. This is important because it is part of the cycle of life.

At some point you and I will physically die. Our bodies will cease functioning, for whatever reason, and begin to decay. This is a natural part of life, and it's essential because what dies ideally goes back into the biosphere and becomes part of the building blocks of life again. Our spirits or souls go to wherever they go and life continues on. When we can accept that this is the natural part of life we won't cling on to the physical body when it's time to die. Instead we will let go, knowing that this is part of the natural cycle. Where people get tripped up is that they try to resist that cycle out of fear or a desire to maintain a physical body forever. Taking care of yourself is important and is something we ought to do, but we shouldn't try to hold onto the semblance of life longer than is healthy.

One of the benefits of working with the elementals is that they teach us to welcome the natural rhythms of life and accept that we are finite beings. I think one of the best ways this can be illustrated is in the act of decomposition. If you go out into nature or even your yard you'll see leaves on the ground in the fall end winter which are decomposing. They are returning back to earth and what they become ends up giving nutrients to the soil. This creates a cycle of life where death, in whatever form it takes, plays its part in sustaining life overall. The elements play a role in the breaking down of things, as much as any other aspect of life building and we can purposely see evidence of this in the stages of laboratory alchemy where a given substance is broken down and then pulled back together again.

The acceptance of death as a natural part of life is very important because it teaches us to accept that nothing lasts forever. This acceptance, when paired with the elemental spirits, can also help us appreciate the role of elementals in the overall cycle of life, because it teaches us that life is not just meant to continually expand (which would make it a cancer) but rather come to a close at some point and start the cycle up again. With that in mind I want you to do the following meditation, because it will prove helpful with any of the healing work you end up doing.

Meditation on the cycle of life and the elements

I want you to get as relaxed as possible. Sit in a chair or lay down and take a deep breath in through your nose, with your tongue touching the roof of your mouth. Exhale from your nose. For the next few minutes simply focus on your breathing, putting yourself into a deeper relaxed state of being.

Once you are relaxed I want you to contemplate the cycle of life from beginning to end. Choose something, whether you contemplate the life of a human being, an animal, a plant or an insect and allow yourself to contemplate the beginning of that life, the journey of that life, and the end of that life. After you've contemplated the cycle of life once, go back and do it again, but this time do it and integrate the elementals into the cycle of life. What role do the elementals play? What activities do they do? How do they help facilitate the cycle of life? Immerse yourself in all of the details, simply observing and being aware of this cycle of life.

When you are finished with the meditation, go for a walk. How does this meditation shape your perception and experience of everything you encounter on that walk? How does this meditation shape your perception and experience of your life?

Share your answers in the magical experiments Facebook group #WWES.

Healing Yourself with Elemental Energy

Contemplating the cycle of life and your own place in that cycle teaches you something fundamental: You aren't above the rest of the living beings, spirits, or this world we live in. You are part of it. You are living right now, but at some point you will die and your remains will decompose and then contribute to the furtherance of future life. If that seems like a grim perspective, I would urge you to reframe that perspective and consider what a miracle it is that even in death, your physical remains are still contributing to life.

With that perspective in mind, we can now turn toward applying elemental magic toward healing ourselves, either with the aid of elemental spirits or without. If we consider that the elements are part of the building blocks of life than we already know they are part of us, as they are part of everything. Sometimes however we may have one elemental force which is too strong and another which is too weak, or out of balance in some other fashion. Early and medieval medical theory used the four elements of earth, air, fire and water to help diagnose the medical issues of the day and while our medical knowledge has become somewhat more sophisticated since then, there is still some truth to this perspective, because if we have too much or too little of a given elemental energy in our bodies, it can set us up to not be as healthy because we're out of balance.

In modern western medicine, the focus on health is typically the physical body, but we shouldn't separate our emotional, intellectual, or energetic/spiritual state of health from the physical health of the body, because they are all interrelated and when you take care of all layers of your health, then you end up taking care of the rest as well. For instance, I have not gotten physically ill in years, and part of that definitely involved a change in life style, eating less meats and more veggies, as well as making some other changes. But part of that work has also continuously involved doing internal work, working on the emotional, mental, and energetic blockages within myself. As I have dissolved these blockages, I have freed up my internal energy, which in turn has fed my overall sense of well-being and health. I've also described the dissolving practices that you can do and I think if you take a proactive approach to your health this will minimize the periods of unhealthy that you experience.

But what do you do when you are experiencing a feeling of unhealthiness? What I have done is applied elemental magic to the problem (along with getting rest and taking medicine). For example if I get a cold, my body will start manufacturing more mucus because it's trying to dislodge the cold. Aside from getting the mucus out of my body, instead of letting the nasal drip get into my respiratory system, what I'll do is work with the element of air to strengthen my lungs, while minimizing the element of fire in my throat (which will be sore) and the element of water in my nose. I'll also maximize the element of earth to help me fight off the cold. How I do this is that I connect with each elemental energy and adjust it in my body, visualizing little dials where I adjust the level of elemental energy that's present in my body. That visualization may seem whimsical but it works, and what I'll do is create a physical representation to go along with the visualization.

You can either take the elemental portals you've created or create an elemental magic board, where you have either the 5 classic elements represented or an expanded system for the elements. On top of that board you could use a planchette, a pendulum, or some other type of tool that can simultaneously help you divine what elemental energy you need to increase or decrease as well as adjust the elemental energy for you symbolically.

I use a pendulum with my elemental magic board. I will hover the pendulum over each element in order to determine which elemental energy is too strong or too weak. Once I know which elemental energies need to be adjusted, I'll then use the planchette to adjust the elemental energy. I treat the planchette as a dial, where when I turn it left, it turns down the elemental energy, and when I turn it right, it turns up the elemental energy. Some people might be tempted to always turn the elemental energy up, but I don't recommend doing that. As with anything else, you want to use moderation in your work with the elemental energies especially as it pertains to your body.

As you become more sensitive to elemental energies you may find that you don't need to use a physical representation to adjust the elemental energies. Instead what you might do is meditate on the elemental energies and make an adjustment during the meditation. You could either do a visualization like I've described above or what you can do is feel into the elements and make adjustments energetically. To do the latter approach what you'll want to do is call up the sensation of the element and then start working with that sensation, either making it less or more in your body, and in the process adjusting the elemental energy.

How do you determine what the sensation of a given element is? I'm not going to tell you what my associated sensations are, because the sensation I might associate with a given element may not be the sensation you would associate with a given element. Instead what you'll need to do is cultivate your own relationship with the given elements and pay close attention to how your body responds to a given element, so that you know what sensation to work with. Once you have experienced a sensation with an element for multiple times, then you'll want to record that sensation and when you need to adjust the element in your body, you can feel into that sensation and make the appropriate adjustments.

Qi gong and the pore breathing exercises that Franz Bardon developed can be useful for helping you feel into a given element and discover what the sensation, but meditation can also be useful for the same purpose. Whatever method you use to discover how an element feels, it's important you do it consistently enough with the given element so that you can feel the element and know what that feeling is for when you want to do healing work with your body. Below is an exercise you can do to help you connect with how an element feels.

Exercise

Take a deep breath in through your nose, while touching the tip of your tongue to the roof of your mouth. Then exhale from your nose. Do this breathing until you reach a place of meditative awareness. Once you are in that state, focus your awareness on the element you want to feel into. Don't think about the element. You want to open yourself to the element. You can do this by either using the elemental portals you've created, placing them in front of you where you can see them, or by invoking the element into you. Allow the elemental essence to saturate your being so that you can be aware of how it feels. Once you have spent some time feeling into the element, let go of the sensation and thank the element for allowing you to connect with it.

So what do you actually do with that awareness of the element? You'll use that awareness of the elemental sensation to help you work with the health of your body when you want to either increase or decrease that element in your body. Once you have experienced it, you'll be able to draw on your body memory of the element to call it up. You may also find yourself becoming more aware of the element in your day to day health and this will also help you monitor your health each day and make elemental adjustments. You can apply this technique to the five classic elements or work with an expanded taxonomy of elements.

One reason I work with the expanded taxonomy of elements is because I find that it does allow for a greater range of health work in your body. For instance if I work with the element of electricity in regards to my nervous system I can increase, decrease, and otherwise work on the electrochemical frequencies of my body using that element, in conjunction with working with the neurotransmitters as spirits (see my book Inner Alchemy of Life for how to work with the neurotransmitters). If I choose to work with the elements of darkness and light I can use them to help me get better sleep or become more awake. If I work with the element of love, I can draw on that element to help me heal a broken heart or become more compassionate with someone. If I work with the element of emptiness, I can draw on that element to help me achieve deeper states of calmness and stillness, which can help decrease mental stress. The possibilities of health magic with an expanded taxonomy of elements is endless, limited only by our imagination and understanding of what the different elemental forces can do, and what we can do with them.

Let's also apply this to a situation where you are sick with a fever or some other illness. Depending on what the illness is, the approach you take with elemental magic will vary. In the case of a fever your body is trying to make its own environment inhospitable to the virus that's causing the fever. You could maximize the element of fire in your body to help you fight the flu off quicker, but also draw on the element of water to keep you hydrated so that when you break your sweat (and the flu) you are able to bring your body back into elemental balance. In the case of cancer, the approach you may want to take involves starving the cancer, so you could minimize the element of earth, while also drawing on the element of emptiness and/or death to kill the cancer. Again, this work is only limited by your imagination and what you consider to be an elemental force that you can work with.

Share your answers in the magical experiments facebook group #WWES.

Healing other people with elemental magic

Can you heal other people with elemental magic? You can certainly do a healing ritual and incorporate elemental magic into it. If you do energy work, you can also work with elemental energies for the purposes of healing other people. I do recommend first making sure you have permission to do the healing work for the other person and that you determine carefully what their specific needs are when it comes to the elemental healing work you'll be doing. You don't want to apply the wrong element to the person. You could do a divination reading before the healing, or if you have an elemental magic board of your own, you can use that in conjunction with the other person to determine what elemental energies you'll draw on for the healing work.

When doing the healing work, depending on what the person is comfortable with, you could either do the healing directly on them or through some representation or spell work. Regardless of how you do the healing work you can integrate the specific elemental energies into the work by using the elemental portals you've created or and making them part of the working, or by attuning into the elemental energetically and bringing into the healing you do. You'll also want to consider what elements may need to be brought done in intensity. For instance, maybe a person has too much fire elemental energy. You could turn that down while turning up some water energy, or if there is too much of the gravity or magnetic elements, you change the frequency for them while strengthening the frequency of other elements.

One of the ways I like to approach this healing work is by imagining there are dials for the respective elemental energies, for a person. I can turn the dial left or right, either turning down the elemental energy or raising it up, as needed. You'll want to pay close attention to how much you are lowering or raising a respective energy, and also provide some further direction, but if you know how to do healing work then it will be easy for you to figure out what to do. If you don't know how to heal other people, I don't recommend doing this level of work until you've learned at least some other healing modalities and have some experience under your belt. Then you can incorporate elemental magic into you healing work. Anyone who has the requisite experience with healing work will know how to take what I've shared here and apply it to the healing modalities they are already using.

I will note that if you're doing energy work for healing purposes, you can integrate the elemental energy into your energy work by first drawing the element into yourself, using pore breathing, qi gong, or some other method that allows you to draw the elemental energy to you and then redirect it toward the person you're going to heal. Remember that you don't want to store the elemental energy in the person. You want to run it through them for the purposes of helping them heal and then afterwards ground them while releasing any leftover elemental energy.

Conclusion

What I have shared in this chapter is an approach to healing magic based on the elements, but what I have also shared is a glimpse of the possibilities that await you if you work with an expanded taxonomy of elements. Instead of limiting yourself to the classic five elements, it can be very useful to expand your awareness of the elements in terms of how that awareness can be applied to your health. In the next chapter we're going to explore some other practical applications for how elemental magic can be worked with, but I also urge you to devote some time to discovering how you can use elemental spirits and energies for healing purposes.

Chapter 7: Practical Elemental Magic

In the previous chapter I shared how you could apply elemental magic toward healing yourself as well as other people. However, we can also work with elementals for other practical magic applications that help us and perhaps even help the environment around us. I make the last comment with tongue in cheek, because so often the focus of peoples' magical efforts is really around their own desires and needs. There's nothing wrong with that per se, but it is also good to look beyond ourselves and consider how else we can apply magic to the world around us.

Protection

The first area of practical elemental magic is protection. When you think about protection what first comes to mind? Maybe you think of a witch war and people casting curses or getting into a physical altercation with someone. Or perhaps you think of the potential of getting into a car accident or falling or some other kind of mishap. You might even consider less physical dangers. Maybe someone doesn't like you at the office. Applying elemental magic to each of these potential issues can be a useful and proactive to potentially prevent or at least mitigate issues.

Before we get those to practical applications though, there is one thing I want you to consider. How much of this need for protection is in your head? I'm NOT saying we shouldn't be as prepared as possible to protect ourselves, but I am saying that sometimes what we need to protect ourselves from is...ourselves. It can be very easy to give in to one's own sense of self-importance and paranoia, even when there is no cause for concern. A useful activity is to consider how legitimate your concerns are, and to create a facts list versus a perception list. The facts are the simple unvarnished truth of a situation, what the reality of a situation is and what you observably know about the situation. The perception list is your own issues that you bring to the situation, the biases that you have. Writing both lists down gives you an objective record that you can use to get out of your own head and determine the validity of your concern, as well as start to figure out what actions, magical and mundane, need to be taken in order to address the situation. Incidentally, you can apply this exercise to any situation where you decide to do practical magic, regardless of what the reason it and it can help you determine what the realities of the situation are versus what your perceptions and biases are. That gives you a platform to strategically figure out what actions you'll take and how you'll use those actions to resolve the situation.

When you apply elemental magic to a situation for protection, you want to consider what element(s) you will draw on to help you with the situation. For example, if I want to protect my car as best as possible from a car accident, the element I might draw on could be earth or metal. I would draw on earth because it could fortify the car, while metal could help bring mental clarity to my driving, so that I could be a better defensive drive. On the other hand, if I want to make my car less visible to the cops, and thus less likely to get a speeding ticket, I could work with the element of light to make car invisible to cops. In general, when applying elemental magic to a situation, what you want to consider is the influence of the element and what specific attributes you want to draw on that will help you get the result you want with the situation.

If you're dealing with a hostile person, elemental magic can also be helpful for protection purposes. First consider the situation: Is this person magically attacking you, mundanely attacking you, or just hostile but not overt about it. For example, if you work in an office and you're dealing with a boss or co-worker who doesn't like you, what you might do with elemental magic in that situation is going to differ from what you would do if someone is actively cursing you. Let's explore each scenario.

In the case where it's a mundane situation of active dislike, consider first the physical environment. Can you remove yourself from this person's vicinity and will that in and of itself resolve the issue? If you can't remove yourself this is where the elemental magic can come in handy. If you're in an office space, what you could do is set up elemental shields or even put elemental spells in the office space of the person who is hostile. One of the things I've done in the past is place energetic pillows in the space of a person that is hostile toward me, with the intent to soften their hostility. You can add elemental energy to the mix, in order to diminish the elemental proclivities that person has or to help them become more reasonable to deal with. To do that, you need to get a sense of their elemental nature.

If we use the four classic elements as a model then what we focus on is which is element(s) that person exhibits the most. If the person is temperamental then it's likely the fire element. If they are very emotional, it's the water element. If they are intellectual, then it's the air element, and if they are grounded, then they are the earth element. What you would do in this situation is set up the energetic construct so that it lessens the dominant elemental energy, and perhaps even increases the other elemental energies, in order to balance the person out. The one thing you have to be careful of though is the tendency to simplify a person based on the obvious elemental attributes, and this is where applying my model of elemental magic may be more helpful. For example, with the grounded person you could work with gravity or space, both of which could also be elemental energies that are prevalent in that person's personality. In the case of a fiery person, you might also work with light and darkness, or even magnetism or electricity. It all depends on what you consider to be an element and what you observe about that person. Regardless of which model you use, your focus is on changing the elemental balance of that person and making them less hostile toward you, and perhaps even becoming friendlier to you.

If the situation is one where you are dealing with a person that is magically attacking you, then you'll want to consider what the magical attack is and how elemental magic and elementals can be worked with to help you defuse the attack and protect yourself. Of course, you can also if you want to fight back, but I find with a lot of these occurrences that the more you feed into the situation, the longer it continues to persist, whereas if you do what you need to do, you can neutralize the situation and move on with your life. In the case of creating elemental magic protections, what I recommend doing is picking specific elemental energies you want to work with for protection purposes and employing them so that they are activated when someone attacks you magically, and otherwise stay passive. To do this you can invoke the element you want to work and then create an energetic shield for the purposes of protection, infusing it with elemental energy. I would recommend using the pore breathing technique to draw the elemental energy into you and then when ready put that elemental energy into the energetic shield that you've created for the purposes of protection.

Exercise

How would you apply elemental magic for protection? What elements would you draw on to help you for the purposes of protection?

Share your answers in the magical experiments facebook group #WWES.

Cursing

Since we covered protection, let's cover its polar opposite, which is cursing. Typically, with elemental spirits, you aren't utilizing them for cursing magic. The one exception I have found so far is with Djinn, which are fire spirits. I recently started working with the Djinn, after my magical partner mentioned she had worked with them before, for a variety of purposes. One of the things I discovered in *Practical Jinn Magick* was that there are curse spells that can be used with the Djinn. It surprised me a bit, because typically elemental spirits don't seem to operate that way, but as with anything else, there can be exceptions to rules, and perhaps people simply haven't shared how they work with elementals in that way.

In regards to cursing, there is the obvious where you can curse someone else, but I've also seen spell work that's focused on cursing a bad habit in your life (and actually done such a working for myself), so this indicates to me that cursing can be done for a variety of purposes and that it's not always directed at someone else. Nevertheless if you are going to curse someone, I think it's important to keep a couple considerations in mind.

First, how much power do you really want to give this person? You have to feel a real sense of passion around cursing someone, and if you're going to do it, it's because the person has done you wrong and you want some justice, but even so this also means the person still has some influence on your life and perhaps even a karmic connection that such work as this may deepen.

On the other hand, maybe the reason you need to do the curse work is to bring some healing into your life by giving yourself a way to release the pain and trauma this person has caused you and send it back to them with interest. Cursing can be a form of healing because we no longer hold on to things that are otherwise holding us back and that includes experiences with other people, where we need to return the influence that person has had on us, back to them so that we are no longer defined by it.

Second, in my experience, most people are their own worst enemies. I certainly can attest to that reality myself, because I have definitely done myself more harm than any person who dislikes me has even done. Of course, I've also learned from my mistakes and to this day I'm a work in progress, doing my best to learn and grow and be a better person. Not everyone feels that way, nor will they, but doing a curse is definitely a choice that you are engaging in order to address what you consider to be a fundamental wrong. At the same time, a curse can be put toward the purpose of helping a person change their ways, because the curse is designed as a punishment and deterrent. I'll discuss that in more depth in a future book, but I mention it here as an example of how a curse can actually be beneficial.

If you want to learn more about how to apply elemental magic work toward cursing, check out the book I mentioned above as the author does a good job of laying out how such work can be done. When I've done curse work, I've primarily done it by working with daemonic spirits, and so I will cover the topic in further depth in *Walking with Daemonic Spirits*.

Attraction (romantic/career/wealth)

One of the ways that I like to work with elemental magic is for the purposes of attraction. Whether you're trying to attract a lover, new friends, or some type of success in your life, elemental magic can be a potent force that can help you with this process. The first thing you'll want to determine is what your desired result is, because the element(s) you choose to work with needs to fit the desired result. For example, if I'm just approaching the spell with the classic elements, I might work with the element of fire if I want to attract a lover, but work with the element of earth for career success. Depending on the friendship, I might work with any of the elements in order to attract certain type of people.

If I'm approaching the spell using my system of elemental magic, then this expands the possibilities. I would work with the element of love to attract a new lover. I might even treat the experience of lust as an elemental force I could work with for the same purpose. I could also draw on magnetism as an element and of course fire. In terms of career or wealth magic I would work with the elements of gravity and magnetism, as well as earth. For friendship I might use the element of light or magnetism. These are just examples I'm sharing, but you if you are using my modern approach to elemental magic, you can pick the element you are working with and then develop the appropriate spell to draw on its attributes and help you achieve your desired result.

For example, one of my long term wealth magic spells is two magnets I've hung upside down, with metal balls hanging from them. It uses the elemental energies of magnetism and gravity for the purposes of attracting more sales. I've set it up so that each time I have a sale, the sale itself feeds into the work to draw on the elements of gravity and magnetism and create more sales.

When I create an elemental magic spell (or a spell in general) I always focus on defining the result first. I use the result to help me understand what forces I will draw on to manifest the result as well as what actions and tools I'll use to execute the magical working. Let's use an example of career magic work, and apply elemental magic to it.

The desired result is in this case is continual success in your career, which could mean promotions and raises, but also opportunities to work at other companies. This could be a continual working that you have setup, and if you're working with elemental magic, you would want to draw on the elements that could help you generate opportunities as well as promotions and raises.

For the spell, I would suggest using physical objects that represent the elements you're working with and can be actual focuses for drawing on that elemental energy. If you're working with magnetism then having a magnet in your office space would be a good focus. If you're working with the element of earth, you might use a piece of gold or some other type of mineral that represents wealth. In some cases, depending on if your office is in your home or in a workplace, you might not be able have a physical representation of the element in your space. For example, if you're working out of an office space, you won't be able to light a candle if you're using fire as your element, but you could keep a wealth shrine in your home and light the candle there.

Once you've figured out the elemental focus, then you can develop the magical working. Go into your ritual space and set up your magical circle (or sphere in my case) and then do a working where you invoke the elemental energies and spirits that you want to work with. You can use the elemental and spiritual portals to help you connect with the elements, or something else of your own creation. Once you call the element in, you'll craft the spell and ask the elemental spirits to contribute elemental energy toward the spell. I would recommend making the elemental focus be the central part of the spell, as well as something you commit to interacting with every day, since you'll want to put a bit of sustained attention toward it and elemental forces you are working.

For the spell itself, it comes down to doing what makes sense to you. In my case, where I created the gravity/magnetic wealth attractors, I kept it simple and programmed the sculptures to act as wealth attractors. I touch them each day and use that to recirculate the working. It was primarily an energy work creation. You'll want to use what makes the most sense to you, to help you construct the spell. Some people might use candle magic or sigils or do an invocation/evocation or use a variation of Bardon's pore breathing. The key is to come up with a working that best helps you express and define the results.

Finally, there is one other consideration and that involves the mundane actions you will take. Mundane actions create a path of least resistance for your magical workings. They are also important because you need to do some follow through of your own in your everyday life. The actions you take, magical and mundane, pave the way to generate the results you want.

Exercise

Create your own elemental magic spell for protection, love, career advancement or something else. What element(s) would you choose to work with and why? What type of elemental focus would you use to represent the element(s) you are working with? What other magical tools and activities will you draw on for the working? Finally, what mundane actions will you take to support your magical work?

Share your answers in the magical experiments facebook group #WWES.

Conclusion

While the emphasis of this book is on working with elemental spirits, I think that learning how to work with elemental magic and utilize it for practical purposes is equally as important. I've sprinkled that topic throughout this book, but bringing it into sharper focus here is really about helping you see how you can apply elemental magic to your magical workings. What makes elemental magic so versatile is how you can apply it as an additional source for your magical work and how you can integrate the elements, whether it's just the classic systems, or my modernized system into your magical work.

Chapter 8: Alchemical Elemental Working

by Jennifer Gerrity

Elements in Alchemy

Alchemy and Magic are interchangeable and closely connected. Alchemy without magic is simply chemistry. In order to succeed with transmutation, the process must be experienced on a physical level as well as an energetic level.

'As above so below', is a famous a quote attributed to Paracelsus, the 15th century father of modern-day medicine and who we can thank for spagyrics, which is the process of applying the principals of alchemy to the plant world. This phrase expresses the essence of working alchemy not only physically, but philosophically and imparting our own magic in our laboratory work to the substances we work with.

Essentially the alchemical world is made up of three kingdoms, the plant, mineral and metal kingdoms. These basic substances are our starting blocks of material to work with. We work with them through the repetitive process of taking them apart and putting them back together to bring the substance to a higher level of perfection. This is done with the mediums of water and wine through the renderings of these substances as well as the use of fire. The same basic process can be applied to any substances in order to change its form so we can create unique expressions of matter that do not occur in nature otherwise.

In working with all three kingdoms, we easily see they express physically and energetically through the philosophical principals known as Salt, Sulphur and Mercury. Once the magician sees nature this way, by the three principals and how they behave, the world around us can also be understood by them as can the human body and disease.

These principals are not physical; they are ethereal aspects of nature which eventually give birth to the four elements.

Salt is the physical realm, the body and the primal materials. Sulphur is the ethereal body, the soul and our connection to universal forces. Mercury is the intelligence, the spark of life and the connection between the physical and the spiritual. Just as the God Mercury is known to communicate between humans and the Gods, in the lab the Mercury principal performs the same action between the alchemist and the substances they are working with.

No matter what the starting substance is, whether it be water or lead... by the art of distillation and the general principles of alchemy all things in nature can be taken apart into these very basic principals.

The elementals come into play via these principals through all three kingdoms and make up the general building blocks of our work. Everything can be broken down into Salt, Sulphur and Mercury and then further broken down into the four basic elements.

Manfred Junius writes in his book: *The Practical Handbook of Plant Alchemy* "These three Philosophical Principals are accessible to our senses in the form of matter which manifests in four different states: 1. Solid 2. Liquid 3. Gaseous 4. Radiant or etheric. These manifestations are considered the four elements. They are called Earth, Water, Air and Fire, and are endowed with the properties cold, moist, dry and hot." (1985, p. 38)

Water houses the primal spirit of this element which we work with as a fundamental in the lab. Spiritual waters such as those from sacred wells, dew during Spring when the life-force is strong, rain or hail from thundershowers when the niter is vibrant and expressed through storm clouds are ritually collected and stored in incubation. These living waters can be distilled using very low heat into the four elements in order of volatility. When applying heat to a substance, the lightest and most active elements will distill first. The most volatile being the fire element which comes over first, and quickly. Next is the second lightest most volatile or the air element, following by the third, increasing the intensity of the heat incrementally, and then finally we are left with the heaviest fraction being earth.

When working with dew or rainwater the earth element will contain the Gur where actual earth will precipitate out of what started as perfectly clear water. From these four elements, the three principals can be fractioned off and much interesting work can be done with them through the artful process of recombining as the alchemist sees fit.

Magically speaking the alchemist must practice so in the aforementioned process a sense of intention is imparted. The substances are worked with as if dealing with a living creature, one with intelligence, shapeshifting before our eyes. We are an artist, rendering nature from its crude state and changing it into something of a higher frequency and higher intelligence.

Whether we work with plants in the art of spagyrics, minerals or metals, through the kingdoms of nature, we experience the elementals over and over again. They gain in potency and become recognizable in taste and habit. We know them and they know us. This is the true work of the alchemist. A nature magician partnering with the elements in order to complete the great work and bringing forth perfection from one another.

There is the fifth element of course, known to the magician as the Quinta Essentia, or Quintessence. This force of nature is inherent in all things. "It does everything and without it, nothing can be done," says Raimundus Lullus.

Destructive distillation is a method of separating solid substances into their elemental components. With destructive distillation the alchemist is working with very high heat to break down a substance. Often this substance had been pre worked through a series of steps in ways to take it apart and put it back to together, repeatedly.

The magic in this lies in the process itself and approaching all aspects of the work from a meditative mind set. Through this practice, one can ride the energy of the distillation like a surfer rides a wave. All Alchemy is to be worked meditatively. We call upon the spirits before starting a process and ask them to guide us. This can take many forms but always the work is rendered elementally.

It is amazing to witness a solid extract of lead broken down in this manner. The elements behave a bit different under extreme heat than mentioned above. From the solid comes over the water element first with actual water distilling out. This water, or *our mercury* is saved and used for other processes, as it is quite precious and rare. You wouldn't ever think there can be that much water in lead! Water is the mother birthing the other elements. Life starts in water and ends in Lead which is the heaviest expression of Earth and thus the Ouroboros of life is witnessed.

Water is followed by Air which comes over as thick white smoke. Our *'white queen'* representing the air element. Between each fraction is a distinct stop and change in temperature. Thirdly the fire element presents itself. This is a thick fire red oil that begins to bead up on the glass. All of these elements can be seen in the old alchemical engravings with beautiful imagery representing each stage. They are precious to the artist as they are living expressions of the intelligence of the elements to be worked with carefully. They guide our work and tell us we are on the right path.

Once the stinking red oil is finished expressing itself as the element of fire and carefully collected, the original primal matter is calcinated to a thick black coal. The peacock colors presenting themselves in the calcination itself. This is the earth element, the blackness from which all life manifests. The origin and the completion the ouroboros of all things.

The path of the alchemist is to know the elements, to work with them and be guided by them. To attune to the changes from one to the next as the building blocks of life. To work together and apart. Even the physical components of the lab itself can be identified by their element. Fire is the furnace the alchemist heats with. In the old days this was wood fire in a stone enclosure, now adays it is a scientific heating mantle. For calcinations, to burn the body of the starting substance we use flame heat with propane. This fire is essential to all alchemical operations and the skill of the work lies in controlling the flame. From this calcination we receive the Salt.

Air is the vacuum we use to remove oxygen from the distillation trains. This vacuum allows us to boil at body temperature and thus preserve the life force in the materials we work with. The ancients used fish bladders to suck out the oxygen and these days we use vacuum pumps by hand or electric.

Water can be found in our water baths we use to impart gentle heat. The Bain Marie is an essential double boiler to prevent the fire from contacting the work directly. Also, water is found as our wine menstruum to tincture the substance we work with and change them from one form to the next.

The Earth is the physical component of the tools and glassware themselves essential for the construction and operations within the lab, the starting matter and all physical components making up the laboratory itself.

The fifth element, or the Quintessence is the intelligence and life force of the artist themselves; the alchemist and their magic. This intelligence runs through all aspects of the laboratory work and is the beginning and end of all things: to be recognized as a fundamental lifeforce and yielded energetically.

The Elements take on a life of their own in the lab. Alchemists tell tales of the water fractions behaving differently once separated. During deep freezes our fire fraction stays in a liquid state while the others are frozen solid. The air fraction evaporating faster than the others and the earth heavy with Gur and sediment that did not exist before. From this Gur we conjure new life as is seen with the famous homunculus. The magic gives it form but also imparts intelligence and life force from one's own soul.

Once a ginseng spagyric was created under the influence of Mars and with the element of fire as a fundamental aspect. This process brought out the fiery aspect of the root with the intention that it would ignite the fire aspects of the human constitution. The spagyric itself came out blood red and maintained that color even though ginseng tinctures in general are usually a soft yellow hue at best.

The life force element is the spark that makes our work alive. Without it, alchemy is just chemistry. Our new year begins at the spring equinox when the life force is the strongest and there is much niter in the air and therefore in the dew. We deliquesce our salts in this time and perform the most important of laboratory operations, cultivating and yielding this force into our work for the remainder of the year. All magic is guided by the cycle of the year and the elements that make it possible. This work poses endless possibilities for the elemental magician and unique ways to connect with the spirits of the world around us.

Chapter 9: Elemental Magic and Space/Time Magic Work

I consider space and time to be elemental powers in their own right and as we've seen in Dzogchen and Hinduism space, or at least something translated to space in English, is considered to be an element. We live with the reality of space and time every day and they play an integral in the cycle of our lives, the rhythms of life we experience and also the magic we work. I'm currently in the processing of researching what will be a future book on space/time magic, but I thought for this chapter I might share some of the experiences that I'm having with space/time magic as it pertains to elemental magic.

To conceive of space and time as elemental spirits and powers does require a willingness to step away from current scientific notions of space/time as a continuum, so that instead we treat space and time as distinct and separate experiences and entities. I have already begun moving in this direction in my work, because I've found it to be fruitful to explore space and time as discrete and separate phenomena that nonetheless happen to intersect regularly to create our experience of space and time. When we treat space and time as distinct spiritual powers what we discover is a depth to each of these powers that can be useful for elemental magic, because of how we can apply the elemental model to space and time. With that in mind, let's explore each of these elements separately to come to a refined understanding of them in our lives.

Space

When you think of space, what's the first thought or idea that comes to mind? Are you thinking of outer space, or needing space, or a natural space you like to go to? Maybe it's something else altogether. Space is all around us and within us, a part of our reality that is simultaneously the background we take for granted and the environment in which the actions and events of our lives take place.

When I think of space as an elemental force, I think of it as something which encompasses and contains everything else and yet also makes room for everything. In a sense, space is a lot like quintessence, because everything is part of space, yet space is distinct enough to also be its own reality. At the same time, I also consider space to be distinct from quintessence, because it's not focused on combining everything so much as being with everything. If quintessence is the combination of elemental forces to create the element and expression of spirit, space is the ontological existence of things, where nothing needs to be done, all though many things can be done. What is contained within space is both potential and reality.

How do we work with space as an elemental force? In my experience, I have found that working with space is really about making yourself available to be present with space, and take space as it is, without necessarily needing to do anything (until its appropriate to do so). Of course, people are driven to do something with space and the potential of it, and this applies to physical, mental, emotional, and spiritual space. For example, if you move into an apartment or home, the first thing you'll naturally want to do is start unpacking and making the space your own. If you're in a relationship with someone, you'll have ideas about how you want the space of that relationship to unfold, as well as what will occur in that space. And as magicians it should be easy to recognize how often, in the act of creating sacred space, we are also imposing our own ideas, hopes and attachments to that space and what we want it to become.

But what if we took a different approach to space? What if we made room to simply be in a given space, without trying to make it become something else? This sounds simple, but I can tell you it is anything but simple. The fact is we get attached to desires and to the outcomes and results that we want to manifest around those desires.

Practical magic IS results based magic, so it should be no surprise that it can be quite challenging to simply make room for space and be in that space without necessarily doing anything. Yet sometimes the best solution is to be in the space without loading that space up with your desired results and outcomes. After all, when you load a given space up with what you want, you are also taking away from what is actually in that space.

For example, consider a new relationship with someone. You meet this amazing, beautiful and wonderful person that you are falling in love with. You can either load the space of that relationship up with your expectations, desires, and the inevitable disappointments that accompany such things, or you can choose to deliberately be in the space of that relationship and be open to what actually could unfold organically. Most people will take the former approach to some degree or another because it's quite natural to get caught up in your own vision of what you think the relationship ought to become, but if you take the latter approach you open yourself to discovering what the relationship could become, without forcing it. I write these words, but I will say it is easier to say or write this advice, then actually follow it. People want what they want and oftentimes what they want is based more around their own desires than being open to the space of a given experience and letting that experience unfold without too much direction on the part of yourself or other people.

The reason I share this advice about making room for the space of a house, a relationship or whatever else is that when you do this what you are actually doing is allowing yourself to get know that space and let that space communicate with you. I recently (at the time of this writing) bought a house. I'll admit that my initial inclination was to start making changes to the house, but I held off. It wasn't easy! Yet I realized that I needed to make some time to just get to know this space, to discover what it had to teach me about itself. I am learning about this house and the land by simply being with it, without imposing any changes on it beyond the changes that absolutely must be done.

This process of getting to know the space is something that I'm finding to be an exercise in elemental magic, because I am also getting to know the elemental energies and spirits of the house and land, but also connecting to the element of space and being present with it in a way where I'm allowing it to teach me about this new space I find myself in, as well as how to fit my own spaces within that larger space. For instance, my magical partner and I have created a sanctuary space for our magical work in my new home. Creating this space has involved feeling into the large space and working with it to find the best room in the house that could be the sanctuary space. It has also involved getting to know that room and allowing it educate us about how it can be worked with.

When you treat the space you live in and work with as an elemental force you discover how that space speaks to you, moves you and works through you. You realize that the space acts on you as much as you act on it, and as a result you can build a collaborative relationship with your space that empowers you and it, while working with it as an elemental spirit and expression of reality.

Ritual: Working with Elemental Space

Pick a space that you would like to get to know better, and where you would like to connect with the element of space. This can be your home or a specific room in your home, but it could also be a space in the land you live on or a space in a park. Once you've picked the space that you want to connect with, what I want you to do is spend some time in that space. Don't do anything to the space or with the space. Simply spend a bit of time being in the space. Close your eyes and extend your other senses outward to experience the space, then open your eyes and look around the space. What do you notice about the space? What does the space communicate to you?

After you've done this exercise a few times and really gotten a sense of the space, it's time to connect with the element of space, within that specific space. You can create and use elemental portals to represent space for this purpose or you can do something else that allows you to connect with the space. For example, I like to dance within a given space and use the dance to help me connect with the element of space, because the act of dancing is a form of connection and communication with a given space and in this case can also be used to communicate with elemental space. If I'm choosing to connect with elemental space, I might trace the symbol of elemental space with my hands and feet as I dance or express it in some other way that helps me communicate with the element.

Regardless of what action you take to connect with elemental space, the action needs to be something that helps you tap into the power of elemental space, and allows you to express that power within yourself, through you, and to the world around you. What you are ultimately doing is imbuing the space you are working in with the elemental energy of space, so that you can draw on that element, just like you would with any of the other elements.

You might wonder how you would apply elemental space to your magic. I think it can be really helpful to work with the element of space when you need to give yourself some space from a stressful situation. Making space for yourself with the element of space means getting a larger perspective than what you had before. I also like to work with the element of space to help me when I am decorating a space so that I can set that space up with the best magical properties or connect with the currents of energy that are already in that space.

Time

If space is the background of our lives, where events, people, and places are situated, time is the action that moves us to and through those spaces, but time is also an element in its own right. It is another force that moves through our lives and moves us and at the same time it reminds us of the inevitability of our own role in the elemental cycle of life. We are born, we grow up, we grow old, and we die, and start all over again, in one form or another. Yet for many people the experience of time is solely linear, wrapped up in the ticking of seconds to minutes to hours to days to weeks to months and so on and so forth. This is clock time and it's something which has replaced the more cyclical aspect of time that our ancestors lived by, and that some people still observe.

Even though I have experimented a lot with different states of time consciousness, I myself have recently come to acknowledge a much more cyclical aspect of time by observing the full and dark moon as well as the wheel of the year. I had never really observed the wheel of the year previously, but my magical partner does observe it because it is part of her spiritual path and in observing it with her, I've come to recognize that I had missed something fundamental in my space/time magic work. Observing the wheel of the year and the rhythms of the sun and moon has a powerful effect on a person's sense of time, because it takes you out of a strictly linear everyday experience of time. Instead you connect with the natural rhythms of time as expressed by a grounded experience of how light and dark change with the passing of the seasons and the progression of life throughout the year.

Of course, there are other ways to experience an altered state of time consciousness. Entheogens, whether through alcohol or other substances, can alter your sense of time, although you also lose a certain degree of control with the substances. There's also states of consciousness such as hypnosis and flow, which create a different sense of time and anyone who's done a substantial amount of magical work has undoubtedly experienced a state of sacred time where time either seems to slow down or speed up. There's also different variations of time experience based on the culture you live in. Some cultures have monochronic time where everything is very linear and clock based and each event is spaced at one distinct moment in time and other cultures have polychronic time where multiple events are happening at the same time. All of these different experiences of time point to the fact that to some degree time is perception based (particularly the measurement of time) but also just how prevalent time is within our lives. We define our lives around time, and around how much of it we have or don't have. If that's not an elemental force, I don't know what is.

Our experience of time is also action based in the sense that the actions we take, or lack thereof define the experience of time that we have. For many people the experience of time is defined by the work week and the weekend, but it can also be defined by various other activities that we do. In one sense, we do the activities that we do to fill up that experience of time, but in another sense the experience of time creates the activities that we do. If this seems a bit paradoxical, just consider that time itself and our experience of it is also paradoxical. What I mean by that is that we simultaneously live in the past, present and future at all times. We experience the past through the memories that we have, the joy and regret we feel around past experiences, and what we learn from the past. We experience the present in our everyday lives, living in each moment as it occurs, but also projecting ourselves into the past and future. We experience the future in the projection of our hopes, dreams, fears, and disappointments, all of which allow us to fantasize about what might be (though how we turn what might be into reality involves taking action).

We also experience time sideways, in considering the possible life paths we might have taken and the time lines/webs we might have experienced. We experience these possibilities through our dreams and imagination, showing us what could have been if we made a different choice here or there. Sometimes we even end up stepping from one timeline to another though usually such a choice is a result of radical actions that change the direction and focus of our lives.

My point in sharing all of this is that time interweaves itself throughout our lives, shaping and building our lives, moving us along even as we try to move it. Learning to work with time magically as an elemental spirit can be quite useful because it opens us to the hidden potential of the universe and perhaps gives us a bit more control or at least an illusion of control that we might otherwise miss out on. When we understand that time is an elemental force it teaches us something essential, namely that there are multiple ways to experience reality and that the only limit to experiencing reality in its various forms is the one we impose on ourselves.

Ritual: Working with Elemental Time

If you want to get know time as an elemental force, it's useful to do some work around your perception of time. For this work, I would recommend picking a period of time where you will deliberately choose to observe time from a different perspective than your everyday experience. Whatever experience you choose has to be something that you at least dedicate a month to, in order to give yourself an extended experience of time that's different from what you normally experience. For this work though, I would really recommend making a yearlong commitment to experiencing time differently, which may seem like a lengthy period of time, but really isn't in the grand scheme of things. Now before you get too concerned about how much work or time this will take, I want to point out that while you will be observing time differently, this still shouldn't prevent you from living your regular life or pursuing your other activities. The main difference is that what you're seeking to do is cultivate a different experience of time, which enables you to better appreciate and work with it as an elemental force.

For example, at the time of this writing I have committed to observing the cycle of the year, both in monthly full and dark moon rituals and in the Pagan holidays. Making the choice to observe the wheel of the year has allowed me to connect with a deeper perception and experience of the cyclical nature of time. It's helped me reach some breakthroughs around the power of iteration, where activities are done again and again and again, with an awareness of how iteration can become part of a cyclical expression of time. If you've never observed the wheel of the year or something similar along those lines, this could be a good way for you to challenge your perception and experience of time.

Speaking of iteration, another approach to this time exercise can be found in doing the same daily magical working again and again. For instance, I do the Sphere of Art each day, which is an invocation of the elemental archangels as well as the archangels of space/time (my version of it). I have created magical art that I use in conjunction with this work to help with the calling in of the archangels, but also to help attune the energy of the space and time I work in. Doing this work each day creates its own experience of time, with each magical working being a reference to the present, but also the past and future, tying together iterations of each experience to empower the overall working. It also creates a rhythmic experience of time around the activity of the ritual and the ripples that spread outward from doing it.

The elemental balancing ritual that I shared earlier in this book is another example of a working you can do that will alter your perception and experience of time. Making the choice to work with an element for a year causes you to focus on how that element shows up but it also changes your experience of time because the focus is on experiencing that element within a very specific time frame and that timing defines the element, but also defines you.

There are other variations of time you can work and I've covered these extensively in my *Space/Time Magic* series. For this ritual I want you to pick an experience of time you can commit to from the examples I shared above or in my other books, or from your own experience, but make it something you can commit to that will help you deepen your understanding wand experience of time as an element.

The Intersection of Space and Time as Elements

Space and time are interwoven together. While we have considered them as separate elements, they nonetheless come together and can't easily be separated from each other, especially because they occur in context to each other. Space provides the stage that the action of time occurs within, while the action of time turns the possibilities of space into the manifested identity and reality that makes the space what is, while also offering tantalizing glimpses of what it could be.

When you work with space and time as elements, what you are seeking to do is take the action of time and apply it to the ontological realities of space so that you can change your identity and the identity of that space. You align the elemental forces together to create a new identity for yourself and the space, and leave behind your old identity. Many magicians will not think of space/time magic in this way, because in the West so much of the focus is on doing something, instead of being something, but learning to become your next identity through the alignment of space and time teaches you just how much the act of doing originates from the identities you've assumed and taken on. When you can shed one identity for another you've learned how to step through space and time to become what you need for when you need it.

Space and time naturally intersect already. What the magician brings to the equation is the assumption of identity and the ability to tap into and call forth the possibilities that are needed to make that identity reality. I've covered various techniques for doing this in other books, but if we want to apply an elemental model to this work then what you can do is cultivate a relationship with elemental space and elemental time, much like I've described with the other elements. The exercises above will help you, but you can also create elemental portals for space and time and use them in your ritual workings to connect with the elemental energies and bring them into your magical working. Pictured below are the portals I've created for space and time. My element of space has the colors of blue, purple, and red, while my element of time has the colors of black, white, yellow, blue, and brown. You can come up with your own design, but this illustrates how a representation of the elemental force can help you connect and tap into that elemental force and make it part of your working. I would suggest creating mini portals that you can bring with you when you want to draw on those elements or hang them in your ritual space, but remember that moreso than any other elements you already have access to space and time. They are an intimate part of your life that you live with each day and so it's really just a matter of opening the doors of your perception and unlocking the possibilities that already exist and that you've never noticed until now.

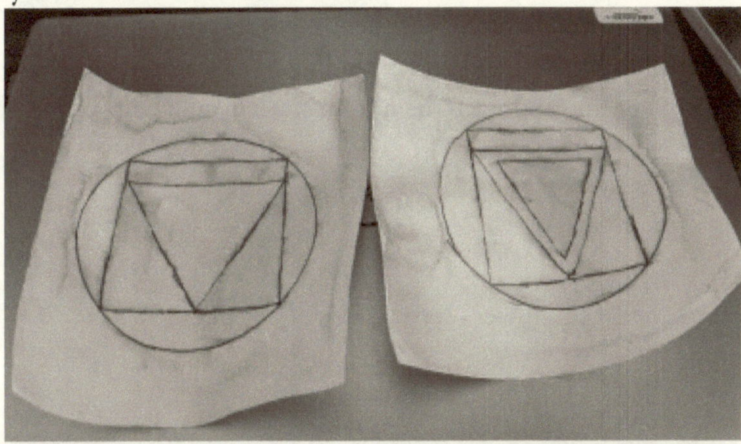

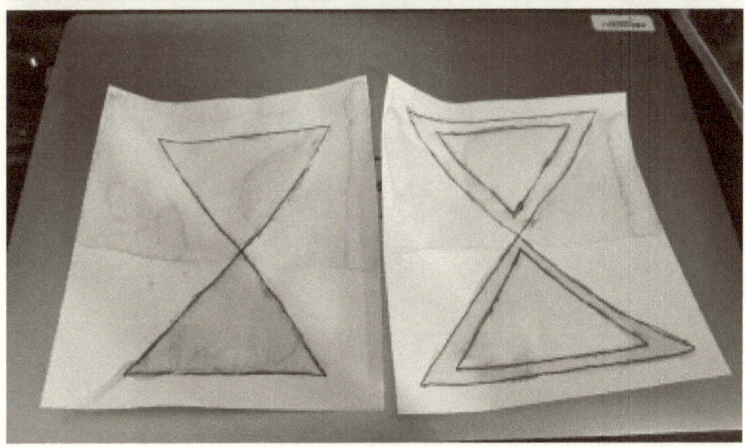

Conclusion

We've explored how space and time are distinctive elements in their own right. While I could have included these elements in a previous chapter, I opted to devote a specific chapter to them, partially because of my previous writing, but also because I think that these two elements are taken for granted moreso than others because they are so prevalent in our lives. We live in space and time and are defined by both, but many people rarely take the opportunity to explore alternative definitions of these elements or find a way to work with them that creates a more proactive relationship. It's my hope that this chapter has given you some food for thought, especially if you have opted to do the exercises. If you haven't done them, consider doing them and seeing how your relationship and understanding of time and space change as a result, when you approach them from an elemental perspective.

Chapter 10: Q and A Chapter

This is one of my favorite chapters of any book to write, partially because it means I'm at the end of the book, but also because I get a chance to answer questions that people asked about the topic. I hope you find the answers helpful!

Why would I choose to work with elementals?

Elementals are relatively friendly spirits to work with and easier to connect with than other spirits. They also teach you a lot about the world and universe and how important it is to connect with the world in a meaningful way. They were the first spirits I worked with and I would recommend that anyone start with them, because of what you'll learn in terms of working with spirits, and because it will teach you a lot about the fundamental nature of the world and how to recognize and work with elemental energies. I figure if you've read the entire book you've also come up with some other reasons for why you would work with them.

How can I work with elementals effectively?

There a few key points to keep in mind when working with spirits of any type, including elementals. The first point is that I highly recommend approaching elementals from a place of respect and mutual collaboration. Remember that what you bring into the relationship and interaction with the elemental spirits is what will be mirrored to you by them. For example if you approach them with fear, then they will mirror that for you. Elementals in particular work on the emotional level because they are more primal in their nature.

The second key point is to have a very clear understanding of what you want the elementals to do for you. Regardless of how you convey that request to them, it's important that you have that understanding before contacting them, because this will make your spirit work more effective.

The third key point is to make appropriate offerings. You can determine what those offerings will be when you contact the elemental spirit by finding out what it is they want to receive from you. Once you know what they want, follow through on your offering.

A fourth key point, particular to elementals is that there is a tendency to sometimes think elementals are simple or less sophisticated in comparison to other spirits. I haven't found this to be the case. If anything what I've found is that the elementals are very focused on their specific functions and within that function they are very intelligent and can be helpful. If you remember that about the elementals, it can help you get more out of the relationship with them, because you'll be working within their zone of genius.

Ultimately to work with elementals effectively, you need to consider what their nature is and how they function and then plan your magical work around that so you can work with them in a way that helps you achieve your goals and at the same time benefits them and their function.

Can you put different elementals together in a working? For example could I combine air and water elementals?

There a few different ways you can work with combination of elementals. With the four primary elements of earth, air, fire and water, you can work with other elemental energy in the primary elemental energy. For example you could work with air of air, earth of air, water of air, and fire of air. The different elemental combinations changes the experience of the element and how you work with that energy. If you opt to go with my modern take on elementals, you could also add gravity of air, magnetism of air, darkness of air, etc., into the mix and work with that as well.

The other approach you could take would be simply to call in and work with multiple elemental spirits. You may want to be cautious in taking that approach because even though elementals ostensibly work together, there could be some potential issues with how they work together, so put some thought into how you would set up the working to work with multiple elements of different types.

I do think it can be more effective to work with a given elemental type on its own because of the function based aspect of the element, but there are times where it can also be useful to work with more than one type. For example if you're doing health magic, working with the element of water for the liquids of the body, while also working with the element of earth for the body can help you do targeted work on your body with both elemental energies facilitating that work and strengthening your entire body.

What are the benefits of working with elementals as opposed to working with deities?

The elementals don't necessarily expect worship or devotion, whereas deities may expect that from you. Also deities may assign you specific tasks and activities they want you to do, while elementals will not necessarily have such expectations. I think the chief benefit of working with elemental spirits is that they are relatively easy spirits to work with and don't necessarily have strict expectations. I first learned how to work with spirits by working with elementals and I think they are a good type of spirit to start with. Working with a deity typically brings specific obligations that you choose to take on because you are choosing to become a follower of that deity. That relationship has its own benefits, but it can be good to explore other types of spirit relationships, and elementals are a great place to start such work.

What offends them? Can they turn on us because of miscommunication?

Like any other spirit (or person for that matter) breaking your word and not following through on your promises will likely insult them. I also think its really important to work with them respectfully. No one likes to be disrespected and the spirits don't like it either. When working with elementals, its important you treat the environment respectfully as well, because that is part of what they are and work in and disrespecting it will cause them to become hostile.

A childhood friend of mine once tried to work with a water elemental. He never told me exactly what he did, but he apparently upset it enough that it became hostile and he had to forcibly banish it. He stopped working magic afterwards, because that incident was enough to unnerve him. What that story told me is that he underestimated the elemental spirits, which many magicians do. I think with any spirit contact, you always want to recognize that you are choosing to interact with another being and that being may not have your best interests at heart...in fact often it won't. Every being has its own agency and once you understand this it can help you make more effective choices around how you work with spirits, how you discover what they want, and how you communicate with them overall.

The spirits don't owe us anything and we aren't special or better than them or worse than them. We're simply all beings living in a vast ecosystem and all of us have our own agencies and agendas. Once you recognize this and also recognize that the expectations you have around how spirits interact with you is always going to be tempered by your own biases (which need to be recognized) this will help you realize the importance of discernment with your spiritual connections and the value of recognizing your own needs versus the needs of the spirits and tempering your approach accordingly.

Does an "avatar" mean an individual who can work with all the elemental spirits in a team?

I think you are thinking of *Avatar the Last Airbender*. In the case of working with elemental spirits you don't need to be an avatar. Anyone can work with them.

When I am doing elemental magic for the first time...what are the dos and don'ts?

If you've already worked through the exercises in this book then you've done elemental magic, but just in case you haven't, here's the do's and don'ts:

Do treat the elemental spirits and the environment you are working with respect.

Do understand that the work you do with the elementals is a long term relationship that will evolve with time.

Do your research and develop a solid understanding of the element outside of the magical work you do with it.

Do go for walks in nature to observe the element but also pay attention to the element in your home and work.

Do your ritual work with the elements but also find ways to incorporate the elements into your life in other ways.

Don't assume you are better than the elementals or smarter or that they have your best interests at heart.

Don't be disrespectful to the elementals.

And otherwise…do the exercises in this book and really work them over. Check out the books in the bibliography because there is some really good content in those books with excellent exercises!

What are the major benefits of working with elemental magic and can it be linked to astrology magic?

The major benefits of working with elemental magic is that it teaches you how to connect with the fundamental building blocks of the universe and learn how to work with them in your magical practice. In the process of working with the elementals, you learn a lot about your own connection and relationship the world and universe. You also learn how to work with those forces and make them part of your life, not only for getting results, but also changing your relationship to the world and the elements. Elemental magic is ongoing work and that's how it ought to be when you choose to do magic work. I've been working with elemental magic for 30 years approximately at the time of this writing and I've never stopped working with it. If anything the elements have become an increasingly important part of my life and spiritual path and I think that is the biggest benefit because they have helped me achieve a path of growth and development that has helped me change as a person in ways that I would consider to be overall for the betterment of myself.

As for whether elemental magic can be linked to astrological magic, I would imagine that you could use the timing of the planets with elemental work. I've never done it and I don't think it's essential, but I imagine you could if you wanted to. On the other hand, perhaps that's another major benefit! You don't need to rely on specific timing to work with the elements.

What should you not do with elemental spirits? To clarify, I always see like commentary related to elementals and a lot of magic in general being like, customize and find a personal approach, find what works best for you and almost never I do I see any comments on like "maybe don't do this thing in general, your mileage may vary of course but most reports are bad" etc., so I always have this lingering question of is it a truly infinite approach or is there a line somewhere that just should not be crossed if you want favorable or even neutralish results?

First, use your best judgement, based on your own experiences. That may seem like a flippant answer, but at the end of the day you're the one practicing the magic, so you really do want to make sure that you are using your own best judgement. I've already shared some answers that I think address this question, but I will share them again, because I would rather say something too much than not say it enough.

Don't be disrespectful to the elemental spirits. Approach and work with them respectfully and you'll get better results and achieve better relationships. Also don't disrespect the environment, because you're basically disrespecting the elements. This means don't litter or desecrate the environment. In fact if you want to do something that helps the environment, the elementals would probably be pleased with that as an offer.

Beyond mentioning those points, I will note that magic can be a very personalized experience. You can and hopefully have done the exercises and rituals in this book, but what will ultimately make this work yours is where you take it from here and how you develop your own relationship with the elements and the elemental spirits. To some degree, through trial you'll need to discover what works and what doesn't work. This is true for all of us and it is a continual journey for all of us. Even 30 years into my own practice I find this to be true and I suspect that will be the case down the line as well.

Can you explain the differences and similarities between the elements and the elementals? Also in how you might work either of them together and separately? What can or will elementals work with you on? How do you contract with and honor the elementals you want or feel led to work with? What is the difference between the elementals and other guides and helpers? How do the elementals fit into a current practice?

There is some conflation between the elements and elementals, so this is a really good question to ask. An element is the raw primal force of the universe that comes in a specific form such as fire or magnetism. It is a force that is part of the building blocks of the universe and basically dictates the laws of the universe. We might even think of a given element as being like the law of physics (without overly conflating the two).

Elementals are spiritual entities that represent and mediate the primal force of the elements. They act as intermediaries that we can work with in order to connect with the element itself. They provide us an interface to make sense of the element and are especially useful to work with when we start to connect with elements.

Typically when you start out you'll work with an elemental in order to access the element. The elemental will mediate the energy of the element, making it safe for you to work with. As you become more experienced, you may find that you can work with the element more directly. This has been the case for me, though I must note I made very specific changes to my energetic physiology in order to enable this to happen. I do think it's possible to do more direct work without making such changes, but it involves developing an ongoing with the elements.

As for how you develop that relationship, the exercises and rituals in this book can help you get started with that work, but it also comes down to making a dedicated effort to get to know the elements and work with them regularly. One of the reasons I do my elemental balancing work is to truly get to know a given element and feel its influence in my life so that I can then apply that influence in other ways. Elements can work with you on your health, internal work, external magic for getting results or whatever else you can think of. There are limitations to what they can do and you'll want to consider carefully how you want to work with them, but this caveat applies to spirit work in general. It's useful to remember that spirits, elements included, are great for influencing purposes, but the manifestation end of things is something we are typically better at. Knowing how to work with them to direct their influence can help you immensely when it comes to applying that influence to situations where you want to get results.

I've already covered the difference between elementals and other types of spirits, both in the Q and A section and in the book. How elements fit into your spiritual practice is ultimately up to you. In my case, they play a significant in my magical work. I work with them every day in one form or another and doing that work has transformed my life significantly.

Bardon has an interesting exercise on using the elements to nurture and balance vices and virtues, I would like to see an expanded, more sophisticated, and modernized version of this. Do you have such a version with your work?

I do. This is the elemental balancing ritual that I shared earlier in the book. This practice can be used for the purposes of internal work, and also draws on more elements than just the classic 5.

Are elemental spirits interested in the everyday lives of people?

As far as I can tell, they could care less about our everyday lives. In general I don't think spirits really care that much about our lives, beyond how our lives might best serve their own purposes.

Would an elemental spirit become a familiar to a person if they worked with them for a long period of time?

Unlikely, because you won't necessarily work with the same elemental spirit each time. You might end up working with the elemental spirit of a place but even in that context, the spirit will be an ally you work with, as opposed to a familiar. A familiar isn't the same as an elemental spirit and trying to treat an elemental spirit like a familiar will likely not get you the results you want, because elementals are function based and will not do activities outside of the function they are focused on achieving.

Do you feel elemental spirits related to faery and close to the land? Or perhaps they are more related to archangels and loftier further from human experience- what would be your thoughts on this subject matter? Are elementals capable of protection and attack? What about healing?

I've already discussed this topic extensively in the book, but I'll rehash it here. The elementals spirits are essentially their own category of spiritual being. In typical Western magic hierarchies they are considered to serve the archangels and they may work collaboratively with the Faery and natural spirits, but they have a specific function which is oriented around the work they do with the raw essence of the elements, mediating that essence into the world and universe for the purposes of creating and sustaining life (but also breaking it down).

In my system, I don't place the elements in a hierarchy, but instead prefer to work with them on their terms, by learning how to connect and communicate with them through the experiences I have with the elements. While I think the archangels can utilized as intermediaries for working with the elemental spirits, I haven't found that the elemental spirits are all that averse to working with us directly.

As for protection, attacking and healing, you can certainly work with the elemental spirits in each of those capacities if you want to. I've shared some of these practices in this book, and there are certainly other books that also share other exercises and practices you can do, if you choose to.

How does one acquire an elemental for Theurgic work?

You can't really acquire an elemental. You can choose to work with them collaboratively but they aren't possessions and shouldn't be treated as such, particularly if you want to work with them theurgically, as it would defeat the purpose of the work to enslave or possess an element for the purposes of spiritual refinement. I recommend taking a different approach and considering how to build a collaborative relationship where the elements will work with you to help you attain your goals, while you help them in a similar way.

Does an elemental have the ability to provide long term results?

If you choose to work with an elemental consistently then yes it can produce long term results. They key is to be consistent with your work with the element. Doing a one off working will probably not produce long term results, but continually working with an elemental will.

Want More Spirit Work?

Order directly from me and get your books autographed and shipped to you by me. Order your copies at https://www.magicalexperiments.com/walking-with-spirits

Conclusion

We come now to a parting of the ways. We've walked together with the elements through these pages and hopefully through a span of dedicated time on your part to doing the work that this book prompts you to do. Speaking only for myself, after 30 years of working with the elements, I can safely tell you that I will continue working with them for the rest of my life. Sometimes this work has been challenging, especially when I have applied it toward doing internal work. Yet such work is part of our life purpose and doing it has ultimately been rewarding.

Magical work in general should challenge us and help us grow. It will not always be easy work to do, but it is necessary. Working with spirits makes this work even more interesting because we are interacting with spiritual beings that have their own agency and agenda and yet will inevitably cause us to realize things we need to work on and change, as well as help us with the magical work that we approach them with. I strongly suggest with any spirits that you do this work respectfully and collaboratively. I can't say that enough.

What I hope you come away with is an expanded understanding of elemental magic and elemental spirits, both if you're working with the classic elements or working with my model of elemental magic. Neither approach is inherently better than the other, but both have something to offer you and I hope you will take what is offered and explore it even more fully as a result of reading this book.

It's now for time for each of us to continue our respective walk with the elements on our own paths, but you can always find me online and ask questions in the magical experiments Facebook group. I love practicing magic and I love sharing it with my readers like you. It's my hope that this book has helped you with your own elemental magic work and perhaps given you a different perspective on how to apply such work to your life. The next book in this series will likely be the *Walking with Daemonic Spirits*.

Taylor Ellwood
May 2022
Eugene Oregon

Appendix One: Working with the Land

I think the one of the best ways you can get to know the elemental spirits is through working with the land. When I was a teenager I was given a lot of yard work to do as part of my chores. While I wasn't thrilled to do a lot of that yard work, it and taking long hikes in the nearby parks taught me a lot about the land, and helped me appreciate the power of the elemental spirits. I even deliberately made sure that the far back part of the yard grew wild so that I could work with the elemental spirits there. I also ended up helping my mom with gardening work, which taught me a bit about caring for the land and helped me appreciate life.

If you were to meet me now, you might not think that I was inclined to work with the land, but since buying a house I've been doing some work with my yard, getting to know this land that I'm living on and with. Even though I technically bought the land, I don't really feel like I own it. If anything I feel like I've been given a responsibility and part of that responsibility involves taking care of this land by getting to know it. Almost each weekend since I've bought my house, I've been working on the land, bit by bit and in the process I'm starting to get to know the life that exists on this land.

I'm not in a huge rush to make changes to this land that I'm living on. I recognize I first need to get to know it and let it teach me about itself. When it gets warmer out, I'm going to spend a couple nights under the stars so I can meet the land at night. Even recently, I did an exercise, where I walked outside with a flashlight and turned it on and then turned it off, allowing my eyes to adjust to the light difference. The point of this exercise was to allow myself to notice the difference between the light and the dark, but I also found that it helped me appreciate the land in a different way than I might have otherwise. It caused me to pay attention to what my other senses had to share about the land and the spiritual powers present in the land.

You may not have access to land of your own. You might be renting an apartment or living in a city with access to a few parks, but even in such a case, the elemental spirits are present and you can get to know them by working with the land. Working with the land could involve picking up litter or doing some other activity to take care of the land you are sharing. It could involve gardening and developing a relationship with the plants that are on the land. It could involve taking walks and getting to know the land through the walks you take.

Regardless of what you do, I think it's important to do some type of work with the land, and use that work as a way of helping you develop a deeper relationship with the elemental spirits, as well as with nature spirits in general. The insights you will get out of such work will help you appreciate the elemental and nature spirits, and learn how to work with them better, as well as be more receptive to them. It also teaches you the importance of giving to the land, instead of just taking from it and this last point is particularly important because we have drifted away from a sacred relationship with the land to a relationship that is much more exploitative and less appreciative of the land and what our role ought to be. The only way we can come back into right relationship with the land is by actually taking the time to get to know it and allow it to speak to us and with us, through both the work we do with the land and spiritual emissaries, such as the elemental spirits, who can help us achieve a better and deeper relationship with the land.

Appendix Two: The Periodic Table and the Elements

One of the questions that came up when I started writing this book is whether I've worked with the periodic table elements as elemental powers. As I noted at the beginning of this book there's an actual tarot deck called the Elemental Hexagon deck which uses the elements of the periodic table for the deck. I love that deck and use it regularly in my divination and practical tarot magic practice.

Could you work with the periodic table of elements as actual elemental spirits? Let's consider the criteria involved. If we use the definition of the elements as being the building blocks of life, then the period table of elements fits the bill, because those elements essentially are the building blocks of life. If we use my definition of the elements being something that moves you, then it may be a bit harder for them to fit the bill, but even so I think it could still apply.

Perhaps the most important criteria though is the one you choose to apply to the periodic table of elements. If it makes sense to you work with the periodic table as elemental powers and spirits, then there's no reason not to try. If you think about it the periodic table could basically be a grimoire of the natural and human made elements that can be worked with, much like how you'd work with any other grimoire of spirits. And just like any other grimoire, what you would need to do is form relationships with those elements, cultivate those relationships and learn how to work with the periodic table of elements for the specific purposes that are relevant to the given elements. Naturally you'll want to also do some research into the periodic table of elements, but that's part of what all this work is about.

Now some readers may feel aghast at this idea of working with the periodic table of elements as a grimoire of elemental magic, arguing that this strays very far indeed from what elemental magic is or what elemental spirits are, but since the whole purpose of this book has been to open you to a new model of elemental magic, why not take it a step further and work with the periodic table of elements? What will really stop you? The censure of other people is really a reflection of their own inability to see beyond the conventional and consider the full range of possibilities that are available to all of us. What will really stop you is yourself, and you can make the choice to do something different, and determine for yourself if working with the periodic table of elements, or my modernized system of elemental magic is viable, or if you should stick with the old model of elemental magic. No one else can make that decision, but you.

I haven't worked with the periodic table of elements, but I definitely see how it could be a viable model of elemental magic and as I write this appendix I'm already considering creating a grimoire for that very purpose. Whether I do end up creating the grimoire or not, the fact is there's no reason not to explore working with the periodic table as a possible spiritual practice. If it's something that calls to you, I say experiment with it and see what happens. The worst that can happen is that you'll come away with a much more comprehensive knowledge of the periodic table and a better understanding of what does or doesn't work for you magically. I think such resultant knowledge is priceless and worth the investment of time, don't you?

Bibliography

Abram, David. (1996). *The spell of the sensuous*. New York: Vintage Books.

Abram, David. (2010). Becoming animal: An earthly cosmology. New York: Vintage Books.

Alexander, Christopher. (2002). *The phenomenon of life: An essay on the art of building and the nature of the universe.* Berkeley: The center for environmental structure.

Andrews, Ted. (1993a). *Enchantments of the faerie realm: Communicate with nature spirits and elementals.* St. Paul: Llewellyn Publications.

Andrews, Ted. (1993b). *How to meet & work with spirit guides.* St. Paul: Llewellyn Publications.

Bardon, Franz. (2001). *Initiation into hermetics.* Salt Lake City: Merkur Publishing, Inc.

Barrabbas, Frater. (2021). *Elemental powers for witches: Energy magic simplified.* Woodbury: Llewellyn Publications, Inc.

Connolly, S. (2018). *Daemonic prosperity magick: A practical guide for daemonolaters.* Arvada: DB Publishing

Dominguez Jr., Ivo. (2008). *Spirit speak: Knowing and understanding spirit guides, ancestors, ghosts, angels, and the divine.* Franklin Lakes: New Page Books.

Dominguez Jr., Ivo. (2021). *The four elements of the wise: Working with the magickal powers of Earth, Air, Water, Fire.* Newburyport: Weiser Books.

Ellwood, Taylor. (2020). *Walking with spirits: How to work with spirits and get consistent results.* Portland: Magical Experiments Publications.

Frantzis, Bruce (2012). *Taoist sexual meditation: Connecting love, energy and spirit.* Berkeley: North Atlantic Books.

Gray, William G. (1980). *Magical ritual methods.* York Beach: Samuel Weiser, Inc.

Gray, William G. (1984). *Inner traditions of magic.* York Beach: Samuel Weiser, Inc.

Hargrove, Corwin. (2018). *Practical jinn magic: Rituals to unleash the power of the fire spirits.* Self-Published.

Junius, Manfred M. (1993). *The practical handbook of plant alchemy: An herbalist's guide to preparing medicinal essences, tinctures, and elixirs.* Rochester: Healing Arts Press.

Mace, Stephen. (1998). *Nemesis and other essays.* Milford: Self-Published.

Mitchell, David S. (2008). *Evil: Our dance partner through life.* In Paul O'Leary (ed). *The inner life of the Earth: Exploring the mysteries of nature, subnature, & supranature.* Great Barrington: Steiner Books.

Pogacnik, Marko. (2007). *Sacred geography: Geomancy: Co-creating the earth cosmos*. Great Barrington: Lindisfarne Books.

Pogacnik, Marko. (2009). *Nature spirits & elemental beings: Working with the intelligence in nature*. Rochester: Findhorn Press.

Pogacnik, Marko. (2016). *Universe of the human body with gaia touch body exercises*. Great Barrington: Lindisfarne Books.

Raven, Susan. (2012). *Nature spirits the remembrance: A guide to the elemental kingdom*. Forest Row: Clairview Books.

Rinpoche, Tenzin, Wangyal. (2002). *Healing with form, energy, and light: The five elements in Tibetan Shamanism, Tantra, and Shamanism*. Boulder: Snow Lion Publications.

Stavish, Mark. (2018). *Egregores: The occult entities that watch over human destiny*. Rochester: Inner Traditions Publishing.

Stewart, R. J. (1990). *Music power harmony: A workbook of music & inner forces*. London: Blandford.

Stewart, R. J. (1990). *The spiritual dimension of music: Altering consciousness for inner development*. Rochester: Destiny Books.

Stewart, R. J. (2008). *Sphere of art*. Arcata: R. J. Stewart Books.

Svoboda, Robert. (2013). *Vastu: Breathing life into space.* New York: Namarupa.

Swain, BJ. (2018). *Living magic: A guide to magic in a world of spirits.* Baltimore: Self-Published.

Tyson, Donald. (2020). *Kinesic magic: Channeling energy with postures & gestures.* Woodbury: Llewellyn Publications.

Learn why your spells aren't sticking…and what to do to start getting results

Trying to figure out what isn't working with your magic feels intimidating because there's so much to track.

Let's make this easier for you.

Stop guessing and start taking action with our FREE guide Why your spells don't stick

Scan the qr code to get the ebook.

Discover how easy meditation can be.

If you've ever felt like you can't meditate or you're doing it wrong, get our free ebook Meditation Made Easy and learn

- What's really stopping you from meditation (it's not you!).
- How to make meditation easier to apply to your life so you can get meaningful experiences.
- 5 simple meditation practices you can learn today that will show you results.

Scan the qr code to get the ebook.

Transform your Identity in a Reality Weaver Session

In this one on one conversation, we go straight to creating the magical identity that allows you to step from the present you into the future you with effortless ease.

Stop hoping reality changes. Start designing it.

In 90 minutes you will:

- Get clarity and direction on a major life decision, so you can create your desired reality with confidence and purpose.
- Discover the optimal magical and mundane solutions so you can apply them to transform obstacles into opportunities.
- Step into a different timeline, where what you want to manifest is already real.

Sign up for a Reality Weaver Session with Taylor by Scanning the QR Code:

Get to know Taylor Ellwood and Sheena Witter, your guides to a magical life

Taylor Ellwood is the original magical experimenter. He's developed multiple systems of magic and written a number of cutting edge occult books, including *Pop Culture Magick*, *Space/Time Magic*, *The Process of Magic*, and *Walking with Spirits*. His work is grounded, innovative, and relentlessly practical, offering tools that bridge the gap between the seen and unseen.

Sheena Witter is a ritualist, strategist, and weaver of realities where magic, leadership, and transformation entwine. She serves discerning founders, creators, and visionary leaders ready to reclaim their attention as a sacred, erotic force—one that leads, creates, and seduces with precision.

For books, coaching, and other offerings, visit Magical Experiments.

Bonus Chapter: What is Social Media Magick?

Before I answer the question that is this chapter title, I want to take a moment and define what social media is. While it may seem like a no brainer, I think it's important to define social media itself, because we're dealing with a specific medium of communication and that is what social media is. Social media are online communication platforms that people use to share their status updates, pictures, videos and other content, as well as comment, like, and share the content that other people share. Examples of social media platforms are Facebook, Instagram, Pinterest, Twitter, Linkedin, YouTube, TikTok, and many, many more such sites. Some of these sites have been around for a long time, such as Facebook and Linkedin, and others like TikTok, are relatively new, but gaining popularity and interest all the time.

All of these sites are setup with algorithms which are simultaneously used to curate the content you see and interact with it, while also being used as a way to gather data and predict your behaviors and choices. If that last part scares you, you're not alone because it is rather scary when you consider how our data is being gathered and used in order to predict behaviors, determine what ads to show us, and otherwise try to curate the experiences of life we have. Yet social media, and technology in general is virtually impossible to ignore or opt out of. It has become an increasingly prevalent part of our lives, and while some people may live off the grid so to speak, most people don't and won't forgo the benefits that social media brings along with the downsides of it.

I didn't have access to a personal computer until I was 18 and that computer belonged to my mom. I didn't have a computer of my own until my mid-twenties and it was a hand me down computer. Now though we live in an age where the phones we use have more processing power and bandwidth than the computers I had access to over twenty years ago (at the time of this writing). What we also have access to is all the different types of social media, because there's usually an app on your phone for each of them.

Social media evolved from the bulletin boards, chat rooms, and blogs that were popular in the late 1990s and early 2000s, which typically only net savvy people used. Now almost anyone can use social media and its more rare to find someone who doesn't. What this all means, as it pertains to magick, is that there is a level of reach when it comes to connecting with other people that is unprecedented, but that reach is still not quite the same as in-person connection and communication and probably never will be. While it is possible to have thousands of "friends" on social media, you'll likely only get soundbites of those people lives, and in most cases those sound bites will be filtered by what the person chooses to present to you.

I've given you a definition of social media. It may not be the definition you would use, but for the purposes of this book, let's just agree to operate with this definition for now. You can always add your own twist to the definition, which you more than likely will, because no definition is set in stone. Now that we've defined social media, let's explore the intersection of social media and magick.

What is Social Media Magick?

If you're skeptical that there's such a thing as social media magick, you aren't alone. When I asked people what questions they had about the topic of social media magick (see the Q and A chapter) some of the questions I got were ones where the questioners were naturally skeptical and asking if such a thing as social media magickk could even work. And I get why they would ask, because social media is an online forum of communication and magickk isn't something we typically associate with social media, beyond the occult groups you find on a given social media forum. Yet I would argue under the right circumstances magick can be applied to any discipline and any technology and when it is what we discover is that magick isn't limited to a specific trope or set of symbols and tools, but rather is an extension of the practitioner and the way that practitioner understands how magick works.

For many magicians, social media magick might not be something that does work, because it's not something which fits under the aegis of magick to those magicians, but for many other magicians social media magick does work and makes sense because of how they practice magick. In my own experience, there really isn't a right or wrong way to practice magick. Rather magick offers potential to any practitioner, provided they understand how magick works and can translate that understanding to the medium they are using to practice magick.

In the case of social media, I have found it helpful to apply several different lens or models to social media to make it adaptable to magical work. The first model is the psychological model, which in context to social media looks at how the psychology of the practitioner and/or other people can be affected through the medium of social media. The second model is the information model, which in context to social media explores how the algorithms can be worked with and manipulated in favor of the magician. The final model is the energy model, which in context to social media looks at how attention and action taken by people can be transformed into fuel for magical workings. We could even apply the spirit model in the sense that social media can be another portal for spirits to work through, influence and connect with us. Of course, these models are just filters, but they are useful ones that you can apply to a given medium in order to appreciate how that medium can be worked with.

So what is social media magick? Social media magick is the practice of magick using social media as a medium of expression for that magical work, in order to get results of some type, either practical or spiritual that benefit the practitioner. This practice of social media magick utilizes the medium of social media in combination with more traditional practices in order to help the practitioner get meaningful results, and it incorporates the available technology as part of that magical process.

It's a simple enough definition, but let's unpack it a bit. When we think about magick as a practice perhaps what comes to mind are the magical spells or the ritual tools or the work with spirits, all of which are valid expressions of magick. Yet what we need to keep in mind is that these are expressions but not what magick actually is. Magick is ultimately a process by which a person manipulates the potential to turn it into manifest reality. There are numerous expressions for accomplishing that and what we should mainly be concerned is with the efficacy of those expressions and if we can achieve meaningful results.

In the case of social media magick, the expression of magick takes place through the use of technology in a context that nonetheless also calls in some of the traditional aspects of magick. For example a virtual altar to a spirit can be just as sacred and relevant as a physical embodiment of that altar. The main difference is the expression of the altar, because a digital altar takes up sacred space in a different way than a physical altar does, yet ultimately both expressions of the altar are equally valid because of what they do and convey to the world and to the spirit they are dedicated to.

So why do people privilege a physical altar over a digital altar? The physical altar is something that can be directly interacted with in person. It has a tangible presence to it and as such this creates a valuation around it that may cause people to put more value on the physical altar than a digital one. Yet the digital altar, though it may not have an overt physical presence nonetheless has a presence and that presence is used for the same purpose as a physical altar. It also has a distinct advantage, especially for people who may not have the space for a physical altar. It still provides people a way to honor the spirits they work with and creates a space for them to do that honoring in. The difference is that the space is virtual, but why should that stop us from creating an altar and honoring a spirit? It shouldn't and it won't provided we recognize that a virtual altar can be a valid expression of devotion.

Let's use another example, such as an emoji spell or a spell crafted of words on a social media platform. What is a spell? A spell can certainly have a list of physical components, but a spell doesn't have to have physical components. A well woven spell can be words you string together to create an experience or a graphic image you share or it can be a string of emojis that are meant to be read and create a specific effect. The form doesn't dictate the reality of magic, so much as it portrays the possibility of what magic can be, and if we understand this, then it stands to reason that we can make an emoji spell or any other variant of social media magick into something that effectively works because it expresses a path for the magick to work through.

This is a fundamental truth of magic that is ignored too often in the zealous of form over substance. Magick works because you provide a path for it to work. That path can take many different forms, but the forms do not dictate the effectiveness of the magick, so much as demonstrate how a person understands and applies magick to the world around (and within themselves). If you can recognize this about magick, you can step out of any given form, adopt another, and still be able to get results, because you recognize that the form is not the process or utilization of magick so much as it is a convenient way for you to frame and apply that process to yourself and the world around you.

Social media magick provides us a few different forms we can use and because it does that it enables us to expand our repertoire and adapt our magical work to the online mediums that are most useful to us. Whether that's using a Tiktok or Youtube video, or creating an emoji spell or using a status update for spell work, or creating a meme on social media what it really boils down is that the forms that are used are an expression of the underlying process of magick being worked with and expressed.

Exercise

What's your definition of social media magick? What does it mean to apply magick to social media or social media to magick? What's an example of your own social media magick work that you've done.

Share your answers in the magical experiments Facebook group with #SMM

Conclusion

We've now come up with a working definition of social media magick and in the process I hope have also established why social media magick can be a valid form of magical working. This approach to magick isn't going to be for everyone, but for the people who are drawn to this type of magic, it can be useful to explore some of the other aspects where technology and magic come together, so let's do that now, so that we come away with an understanding and appreciation of social media magick within the context of other forms of technology and magick.

Did you know I also write Fiction?

At Imagine Your Reality, I invite you to explore my fantastical worlds of fiction and make them part of your reality. Whether you're following the adventures of a superhero who's learning how to fly or rooting for a support analyst as he fights off zombies, my hope is that my stories will entertain you and take you to a fantastical place. I write fiction with a twist, because I like to surprise my readers and that's exactly what you'll get with my writing.

That's what Imagine Your Reality is about and I invite you to take a glimpse of the fantastic and read my free novella The Zombie Apocalypse Hospital, which explores what happens when an ambulance driver has to survive the zombie apocalypse.

Visit Imagineyourreality.com to get the free story and get notifications when I publish my fiction.

Learn How Magic Works

In the *How Magic Works* series, you'll learn my process of magic system, which explains how and why magic works in easy to understand language and helps you get consistent results that transforms your life. The entire series is designed to walk you from the basics of magic all the way up to designing your own systems of magic, as well as showing you how to apply creative mediums to your magical practice.

Available in print and e-book. Visit https://www.magicalexperiments.com/how-magic-works-series to get your copies today!

Learn how Pop Culture Magic Works

Magick for geeks! The how *Pop Culture Magic Works* series I explain what pop culture magic is and share how and why it works. I also show you how to create your own system of pop culture magic based on the pop culture that speaks to you. You'll also learn how to work with pop culture spirits and how to create your own pop culture magic workings.

Available in print and on any digital e-book format. Visit https://www.magicalexperiments.com/pop-culture-magic-series/ to get your copies today!

Learn how Space/Time Magic works

In the *How Space/Time Magic Works* series, you'll learn how to work with the elements of space, time, imagination and memory and learn how to use them to turn probabilities into reality. I walk you through advanced techniques for altering your identity and rewriting your present and future.

Available in print and e-book format at https://www.magicalexperiments.com/space-time-magic-series

Learn how Inner Alchemy Works

In the *How Inner Alchemy Works* series, you'll learn how Inner Alchemy works and how you can internal work to transform your life. I'll show you how to make allies of your neurotransmitters and create a relationship with your body that helps you lie a healthier and happier life.

Available in print and e-book format at https://www.magicalexperiments.com/inner-alchemy-series

[1] See my book The Magic of Writing for how to develop personalized chants.

Don't miss out!

Visit the website below and you can sign up to receive emails whenever Taylor Ellwood publishes a new book. There's no charge and no obligation.

https://books2read.com/r/B-A-MUJG-XNHWB

BOOKS 2 READ

Connecting independent readers to independent writers.